THE *Mercy* King

HOW THE KINDNESS OF JESUS HEALS YOUR SIN, SHAME, AND WEAKNESS

SCOTT SAULS

ZONDERVAN BOOKS

The Mercy King

Published by Zondervan, 3950 Sparks Drive SE, Suite 101, Grand Rapids, MI 49546, USA. Zondervan is a registered trademark of The Zondervan Corporation, L.L.C., a wholly owned subsidiary of HarperCollins Christian Publishing, Inc.

Requests for information should be addressed to customercare@harpercollins.com.

Zondervan titles may be purchased in bulk for educational, business, fundraising, or sales promotional use. For information, please email SpecialMarkets@Zondervan.com.

ISBN 978-0-310-36726-0 (audio)

Library of Congress Cataloging-in-Publication Data

Names: Sauls, Scott author
Title: The mercy king : how the kindness of Jesus heals your sin, shame, and weakness / Scott Sauls.
Description: Grand Rapids, MI, USA : Zondervan Books, [2026] | Includes bibliographical references.
Identifiers: LCCN 2026003317 (print) | LCCN 2026003318 (ebook) | ISBN 9780310367246 softcover | ISBN 9780310367253 ebook
Subjects: LCSH: Suffering—Religious aspects—Christianity | Spiritual healing—Christianity | Forgiveness—Religious aspects—Christianity | Christian life
Classification: LCC BV4909 .S288 2026 (print) | LCC BV4909 (ebook)
LC record available at https://lccn.loc.gov/2026003317
LC ebook record available at https://lccn.loc.gov/2026003318

Published in association with the literary agency of Wolgemuth & Associates, Inc.

HarperCollins Publishers, Macken House, 39/40 Mayor Street Upper, Dublin 1, D01 C9W8, Ireland (https://www.harpercollins.com)

Cover design: Tim Green, Tiny Giant Co
Cover illustration: Shutterstock
Interior design: Sara Guild

Printed in the United States of America

26 27 28 29 30 LBC 5 4 3 2 1

To Donald Miller:
For helping me see more clearly the story God is writing
and for helping me find the courage to step into it.

To the friends who stayed close when I needed mercy the most:
You know who you are.

And to the pastors who keep going, despite the enemy's schemes:
You know whose you are.

The hands of the king are the hands of a healer, and so shall the rightful king be known.

—J. R. R. Tolkien, *The Return of the King*

He saved us, not because of righteous things we had done, but because of his mercy.

—Titus 3:5

CONTENTS

Movement Three: The Hope That Holds Us

Introduction

When Mercy Comes Looking for You

There's a reason most people struggle.

Behind the pace and pressure of modern life, beneath the daily decisions and obligations we juggle, most of us are carrying more than we realize. We carry longings—for peace, for purpose, for connection. We carry hurts—some fresh, some long buried. And many of us, even those who have walked with God for years, carry a quiet sense that something is still missing.

Sometimes we call it exhaustion. Sometimes doubt. Sometimes we're not even sure what to call it. But we feel it just the same.

This book is for people who feel that weight. It's for those who believe in grace, at least in theory, but struggle to weave it into their lives. It's for those who wonder whether they've somehow missed what others seem to have found. And it's especially for those who have been told, in one way or another, that they don't quite measure up—not to people's expectations, not to their own, and maybe not even to God's.

The central claim of this book is simple, but it's not soft: Jesus is full of mercy. And not mercy in the abstract. His mercy is personal. It's pursuing. It's stronger than our shame and more patient than our doubts. The Bible tells us that his mercies are new every morning—and that's not just poetic language. It's a reflection of the kind of King he is. A King who reigns not through fear or force but through compassion and kindness. A King who is moved by our weakness, not repelled by it.

That's the kind of King this book is about.

We're calling him the Mercy King not as a metaphor or a catchy book title but as a way of describing what Jesus is actually like. In a world that often rewards performance and hides weakness, Jesus does the opposite. He draws near to the brokenhearted. He welcomes the weary and the weak. He goes out of his way to restore those others have given up on. His strength is not there to crush us. It is there to carry us.

This isn't a theory for me. It's personal.

For much of my life, I operated from a quiet belief that love had to be earned. I wouldn't have said that out loud, but it showed up in the way I lived—in how I gave myself to ministry, service, and pouring into others. Somewhere along the way, I started to confuse being useful with being lovable. If I could lead well enough, serve and give faithfully enough, keep going long enough, then maybe I could feel more secure and I could know that my life had meaning.

What I didn't realize was how, bit by bit, that mindset was wearing me down. Over time, sincere devotion turned into anxious striving. Joy was replaced by pressure, and rest by workaholism. What began as faithfulness started to feel more like fear—the fear that if I stopped moving, everything might come undone, including me.

Eventually, it did. The weight became too much. And when I was at the end of my strength, something happened I didn't expect: Mercy came looking for me.

Not with a list of corrections. Not with disappointment. But with an invitation.

It was as if Jesus himself whispered, "You can stop now. You can rest. You don't have to carry this anymore. You are not alone, and you never have been."

I had spent years preaching this message to others, and plenty of good fruit came from it in *their* lives. Those years were not a waste. But now Jesus was speaking it to me. Not because I had earned it but because I hadn't. And because his mercy really is for the tired and spent. For the ones who are ready to admit they need it.

That realization softened me. It changed how I saw Jesus, how I saw myself, and how I now show up in ministry and in the rest of life. It gave me space to breathe, laugh, rest, and play again. And it led me to write this book.

The Mercy King unfolds in three movements:

- The first explores *the longings we carry*—our desires for belonging, security, and meaning.
- The second turns toward *the hurts we endure*—the kinds of wounds that often get buried or superficially spiritualized, but never actually healed.
- The third emphasizes *the hope that holds us* when the stuff of life seems shaky—when we're tired, jaded, or even facing the shadow of death itself.

Each chapter centers on the person of Jesus. Not just what he said but how he lived. How he responded to the weary, the guilty, the proud, and the grieving. And how he still does.

If you're tired or worried, you're in good company. If you feel like you've fallen short, welcome. If you've been hurt by church or confused by faith, there's still room for you at the Mercy King's table. You don't have to earn your place. You don't have to prove you belong. You're not here because you got it right. You're here because mercy came looking for you.

Before we begin, I want to invite you to pause for a minute and breathe.

You are not behind. You are not cast out. You are not forgotten.

You are being pursued by the kindest King the world has ever known.

So shall we begin?

Not by striving but by receiving.

Not by chasing God but by realizing he's already running toward you.

—**Scott Sauls**
Nashville, Tennessee

MOVEMENT ONE

The Longings We Carry

ONE

When You Feel Too Broken to Belong

The Mercy King Who Invites You In

> Grace is the very opposite of merit. . . . Grace is not only undeserved favor, but it is favor shown to the one who has deserved the very opposite.
>
> —Harry Ironside, *Full Assurance*

One evening the church where I served as pastor hosted a panel discussion on a topic of growing relevance: Christian deconstruction.

For many deconstruction isn't just about rethinking beliefs and theology, it's about wounds. It's about feeling disillusioned, betrayed, or spiritually homeless. Some walk away not because they reject Jesus but because they wonder whether his people have rejected them. The weight of doubt, disappointment, and shame can leave them questioning whether the church still has room for them. This was the struggle behind our conversation.

There is a faithful form of deconstruction that seeks not to dismantle Christian faith but to recover it. It aims to strip away counterfeit expressions of faith to uncover the authentic, life-giving, biblically rooted truths beneath. During the panel discussion, an artist who is also a Christian shared his personal story of growing up in a church environment that nearly drove him away from faith. He described a culture that was rigid, rules driven, and politically charged, a place where mercy was scarce and an us-versus-them mentality prevailed.

This environment left him teetering on the edge of abandoning his faith.

Reflecting on his experience, he said, "We are all fallen and broken. Like every Bible character, we are a mix of glory and dirt. Where we have made a mess, we as the church should be leading with apology and repentance." He also shared a statement often attributed to Gandhi, one that I have also quoted previously: "I like your Christ, but I do not like your Christians, because your Christians are so unlike your Christ."

Whether or not Gandhi actually said these words, they capture the pain of many who feel like outsiders to grace. The artist's story is not unique; it echoes the ache of so many who yearn for a faith community that feels like home but instead find themselves wandering, unsure where they fit. Some wrestle with doubt, wondering whether church, church people, or God can still be trusted. Others battle shame, believing they've failed God too many times. Still others fear that their struggles, if made known, would invite and seal their rejection. If Jesus is full of mercy, why does it seem so scarce and unreachable?

This struggle—the ache of feeling spiritually displaced, uncertain where we belong, and thereby severed from mercy—is not new. Jesus understood this ache well, and in Luke 15 he speaks to it directly to help those who feel disillusioned find their way back home.

To the tax collectors and sinners who gathered around him—outcasts pushed to the margins by religious gatekeepers—Jesus defied all expectations. Even as the religious leaders muttered among themselves about his unconventional ways and shady associations, Jesus continued to extend his arms to the lost, searching, and fed up. His message was, and still is, clear: No one is too far gone for grace.

Jesus didn't just accept tax collectors and sinners, he went out of his way to seek them. He shared meals with them and extended a kind of warm, unapologetic hospitality that was unheard of at the time. As the Mercy King, he broke with social and religious expectations, offering a vision of kindness and welcome that challenges the way we give, receive, and—like the Pharisees—sometimes withhold the gift of belonging.

The King Who Welcomes Tax Collectors and Sinners

To understand Jesus accurately, we must be made aware of how intently he drew near to those whom society rejected. The tax collectors and sinners who gathered around him were drawn in by a love they had never dreamed of for themselves. Tax collectors, in particular, were justifiably seen as traitors, exploiting their own people for profit with Rome's backing. *Sinners* was a broader term used by religious authorities to categorize anyone they considered morally compromised. Yet despite their deserved reputations—or perhaps because of them—Jesus did not push tax collectors and sinners away. Instead he warmly embraced them.

Jesus is irresistibly drawn to the guilty, lost, and discarded. These very qualities seem to attract him most, revealing not just the skills of a healer but the heart of a King who reigns through mercy. In his teaching and actions, Jesus redefines what kingship looks like. Where earthly kings guard their glory, Jesus gives his away. Where worldly rulers demand loyalty, Jesus offers love. He rules chiefly through grace, forgiveness, and restoration.

Nowhere is this clearer than in Jesus' most well-known parable: the story of the prodigal son (Luke 15:11–32). This parable is more than a tale of rebellion and return; it's a window into the heart of God toward anyone who has wandered, squandered, or lost their way. At its core, it's not only about one runaway child but about the universal ache of separation, the weight of shame, and the radical mercy of a Father who runs toward lost souls to love them back to life.

In a stunning act of defiance, the younger son demands his inheritance, essentially saying to his father, "I wish you were dead." He takes what he falsely believes is owed to him and squanders it in reckless living. His self-made freedom feels exhilarating at first. But when the thrill fades, reality sets in: emptiness, isolation, hunger, and shame. The once-proud son is reduced to feeding pigs. He is unclean by his own doing and, in his mind, unredeemable, stuck in the ditch of his own making.

G. K. Chesterton once said, "Man cannot break the laws of God; he can only break himself against them."[1] The laws of God are rock solid; it is we who are not.

The younger son's collapse is not simply punishment, it is the natural consequence of life apart from the father's merciful rule. Alone in a distant country, stomach empty and dignity in ruins, he prepares and rehearses a groveling speech not expecting restoration but merely seeking survival. What he doesn't realize is that his father has never stopped watching. Never stopped longing. Never stopped loving.

The moment the father sees him on the horizon, he breaks every cultural convention: He runs to his son, embraces him, and interrupts his speech with unrestrained joy. The son isn't punished or put on probation. He's *restored*. Grace doesn't wait for the speech to finish, it rushes in with a robe, a ring, and a feast. The son expected boundaries and berating but instead found belonging.

Jesus tells this story not only to offer hope to those who are wandering and ashamed but also to reveal the kind of kingdom over which he presides—in which power is expressed in a way that causes mercy to triumph over judgment.

The two parables that precede the prodigal son—the lost sheep and the lost coin—echo the same heartbeat. A shepherd leaves the ninety-nine to find one wandering sheep. A woman turns her house upside down to recover one missing coin. In both cases, the lost item holds immeasurable worth in the eyes of its owner. And when what was lost is found, celebration follows. These stories lay the groundwork for the prodigal son, revealing a pattern that we also see throughout Scripture and in everything else that is purely Christian: Grace goes first. It initiates. It rescues.

Where the sheep wandered in ignorance and the coin was helpless in stillness, the Prodigal Son walked away by choice. Yet in all three stories, the message is clear: Our lostness never diminishes our worth. It only seems to intensify the determination of the one who pursues.

Jesus, the Mercy King, tells this story to reframe our understanding of God—and of ourselves. His mercy is not weakness, it is authority made manifest through compassion. It is not mere sentiment but sovereign love that chases down the lost, lifts the shamed, and embraces the weary.

These parables invite us to locate ourselves in the story. Whether we've wandered, resisted, or doubted, Jesus extends the same welcome: Come home. The laws of God are not cages, they are boundary lines inside of which we are invited to flourish. And when we "break ourselves against" his laws, the Father doesn't relish the consequences we bring upon ourselves. To the contrary, he runs toward us to rescue and carry us home.

Drawn to the Worst in Us

Jesus' selfless and loving pursuit of his beloved prodigals runs counter to everything we expect. It defies human logic and reveals the heart of a King whose message and methods contradict the ways of the world. The parts of ourselves that we find most discouraging, disappointing, or even shameful—our worst traits on our worst days—are the very places that stir his affections toward us the most. God doesn't love us in spite of our flaws; he loves us in the midst of them and even through them. We might even dare to say he loves us because of them. Like moths drawn to a flame, God moves toward us in our darkest, most guilt ridden, and despairing moments and seasons.

Consider also the apostle Paul, whose life after encountering Christ was marked by unwavering devotion. He planted churches, mentored believers, endured persecution, and was imprisoned and executed for the gospel. Yet at the end of his ministry, his autobiography wasn't a boast of his accomplishments but an honest confession that remained with him until the day of his death: "Here is a trustworthy saying that deserves full acceptance: Christ Jesus came into the world to save sinners—of whom I am the worst" (1 Tim. 1:15–16).

Not was but *am*—a present tense acknowledgment, even at the height of his virtue, of his never-ending need for grace. Yet this recognition didn't lead him to self-loathing or despair. Instead it stirred him to worship and wonder.

The mercy Paul experienced was more than the removal of judgment; it lifted burdens and empowered him to live freely in the presence and love of God. This mercy is not an award for performance but is given freely to those who finally stop trying to perform. It sets Christianity apart from every other philosophy, religion, and creed, freeing believers from the struggle to prove themselves worthy to a God who already loves and accepts them.

It bears repeating: Your moments of deepest discouragement, disappointment, and even self-disgust do not push Jesus away. They draw him closer.

Jesus runs toward you just as the father ran to welcome his prodigal son, interrupting your rehearsed apologies with an embrace that asks for nothing in return. Even the journey home isn't something you have to figure out on your own. Jesus, your Savior and elder brother, is the one who comes looking for you, crossing every barrier, pursuing you to the ends of the earth to bring you back. As John, the disciple who called himself "the one Jesus loved," reminds us, "We love because he first loved us" (1 John 4:19).

And as Charles Spurgeon once said of Jesus' mercy, "There is mercy for the very chief of sinners. Mercy, that has no bounds. Mercy that is infinite. Mercy that is given freely. Mercy that is given even to the vilest of the vile."[2]

Jesus' mercy can dismantle the self-righteousness and contempt of the Pharisee within. When the depth of his love reaches the center of our thoughts, we notice changes within ourselves. Pride gives way to humility, and judgment becomes mercy, transforming us into beggars eager to tell other beggars where the bread is.[3]

I once had a conversation with a pastor from the urban core of St. Louis who offered some thought-provoking insights about the church he served. Among their written core values, one stood out in particular: weakness. At first this might seem like an unusual or even unappealing value, but it's deeply rooted in Scripture. It's the very quality the apostle Paul chose to embrace and highlight when he wrote, "I will boast all the more gladly about my weaknesses" (2 Cor. 12:7–10).

The truth is that we are all weak. We just expend significant effort trying to keep it hidden.

The St. Louis pastor shared a story about a couple who began attending his church. They were in a complicated relationship—nonexclusive, unmarried, and sexually active—and they came to him not seeking moral advice but simply hoping for help to improve their relationship.

At first his internal response mirrored the Pharisee spirit: quick to identify their flaws and trace their struggles back to their choices. But something shifted in him during their conversation. He noticed his own eyes drifting toward the woman's short skirt, and in that moment conviction settled in. "I'm no different," he thought.

That realization didn't disqualify him from ministry; it prepared him to respond according to his church's stated core value of weakness. He was able to respond pastorally, not with condescension but with the compassion of Christ. Instead of becoming a smug, self-appointed gatekeeper, he became a fellow beggar telling other beggars where the bread is, extending the same mercy he knew he needed himself.

This is the essence of Jesus' ministry: meeting us in our mess and moving toward us, not away. Our misery and his pursuit are intertwined. He not only welcomes tax collectors and sinners, messy churchgoers and stumbling pastors, but he also sits with us, shares meals with us, and transforms every table into a place of warmth and belonging.

The Mercy King's Table

When Jesus shared meals with tax collectors and sinners, it was more than a casual gathering. It was a radical act that redefined who was in. Inviting someone to dinner once might be a friendly gesture or a polite interaction that ends when the meal is over. But welcoming someone to your table repeatedly signals friendship and lasting connection. It's one thing to invite someone; it's another to genuinely want them. Jesus' table was not just a temporary refuge, it was a sacred space where a real, enduring community gathered.

Gandhi, despite his admiration for Christ, wrote in his autobiography, "The pious lives of Christians did not give me anything that the lives of men of other faiths had failed to give." He acknowledged the soundness of Christian teaching and ethics but found little distinctive impact in the Christians he encountered. "From the point of view of sacrifice," he noted, "Hindus greatly surpassed the Christians."[4]

Gandhi's critique ought not be dismissed or taken as an offense; it should challenge us deeply. It suggests that what often stands between spiritual seekers and Christ is not Christ himself but his followers. When we fail to reflect the love and grace we have received, it has real consequences.

It's one thing to speak Christ's words; it's another to live them. It's one thing to attend church; it's another to be the church. To Gandhi, the Christians he encountered offered nothing more compelling than what he saw in other faiths. While Christ's life was profoundly captivating to him, he struggled to see it mirrored in Christ's followers.

As the artist mentioned earlier expressed, our way forward is not through self-sufficiency or simply getting our act together but through apology and repentance. From a place of humility, we can reclaim and impart the true essence of our faith not by hiding our failures, weaknesses, and sins but by owning them and allowing grace to heal and transform us.

This is how we dismantle the façade of religious pretense and recover a faith that is both authentic and fruitful.

A spirit of apology should shape the way we engage with others. Patti and I, though far from perfect, have tried over the years to weave this posture of humility into the fabric of our marriage and parenting. We learned early on that pretending to be better spouses or more competent parents than we actually were—standing above correction or critique—only creates distance. Rather than drawing our children in, a self-protective posture places a burden on their hearts.

So we chose as much as possible to take the lower, more honest road. To bring our flaws into the light. To own our shortcomings without excuse. And to invite our kids into the healing moments that so often begin with two simple, trust-building words: "I'm sorry."

I remember one evening when I failed in a way that still stings to recall. I had grown frustrated with one of our daughters and, in the heat of the moment, spoke to her sharply and called her an unflattering name. The look on her face told me everything. Words spoken in frustration, especially from a father, can wound in ways that linger long after the moment has passed. To make matters worse, her sister was there too, taking in behavior no child should have to witness from her father.

That night at dinner, I knew that sweeping it under the rug wasn't an option. So I apologized. To the daughter I hurt directly, because "sticks and stones may break our bones, but words can cut us deeply." To her sister, who had seen it happen. To Patti, who felt rightly grieved that the man she married had spoken so harshly to their child.

And in one of the many grace-filled moments that have quietly marked our family over the years, she forgave me. As she—and each member of our family—has graciously done more times than I deserve.

We've never aimed to be flawless parents. But we have hoped to be honest ones. Parents who model the gospel not by pretending we never mess up but by owning our wrongs, seeking forgiveness, and trusting that love—real love—grows in the soil of humility and grace.

King David seemed to be on a similar track when he wrote, "A broken and contrite heart, O God, you will not despise." God is pleased when we bring our brokenness and contrition not only to him but also to those we've wronged. Jesus underscored this when he said that even worship should be put on hold if there is unresolved conflict we can address: "Therefore, if you are offering your gift at the altar and there remember that your brother or sister has something against you, leave your gift there in front of the altar. First go and be reconciled to them; then come and offer your gift" (Matt. 5:23–24).

Grace is vital for those prone to self-condemnation—wrapped in guilt, covered in shame, and believing we're beyond hope. This is evident in the reassurance Jesus offers to those who fear they have committed an unforgivable sin. The great Puritan John Bunyan, in *Grace Abounding to the Chief of Sinners*, shared that he once thought he had done just that. He described the terror of feeling shut out from Christ because of his own sin and failure:

> And thus I continued a long while, even for some years together. Sometimes I would strive to rejoice in Christ, but I could not; though many times I have at least thus much, "Lord, I will not quite despair, for if I must not trust to thee, yet on thee I will venture my soul." I found it hard work now to pray to God, because despair was swallowing me up; I thought I was as with a tempest driven away from God; for always, when I cried to God for mercy, this would come in, "It is too late, I am lost, God hath let me fall; not to my correction, but condemnation; my sin is unpardonable."[5]

The great Puritan's fear is familiar to many tenderhearted believers who seek assurance and worry that they have gone too far. Yet examining the original Greek in Matthew's gospel, where Jesus warns of blasphemy against the Holy Spirit (Matt. 12:31–32), can bring comfort. The verb for *blasphemy* indicates a sustained, willful rejection, not a momentary lapse or passing doubt. The unpardonable sin is not an isolated act of failure or a slip of the tongue but an ongoing rejection of Jesus' life, death, and resurrection as the source of salvation.

This means that words like *irredeemable* or *lost cause* can never truly apply to you or me. Perhaps this is why God chose to include so many flawed, broken individuals in the Bible: to remind us that if redemption and hope were possible for them, they are possible for us too. When you find yourself thinking, "I'm my own worst enemy," and questioning whether God can forgive you as you struggle to forgive yourself, remember that his grace shines most where sin, guilt, and shame are blatant.

What makes you feel hopeless is what activates his warmth and affection the most.

If you have ever wondered whether you are beyond recovery, take heart: The very fact that you wish for grace is evidence that grace is already pursuing you. Jesus is not waiting for you to fix yourself before coming to him. He is already running in your direction. As C. S. Lewis put it, "Seek him with seriousness, because unless he wanted you, you would not want him."[6]

That pull you feel is his invitation.

It's a sign not of his absence but of his pursuing love.

To reject Jesus' mercy is, in effect, to deny a central aspect of his kingship. A true king not only rules but rescues, and Jesus' ultimate act of kingship was his death and resurrection, a costly invitation into his kingdom. Our struggle with shame and self-doubt is not just about insecurity; it's about whether we will take the King at his word when he tells us we are his beloved.

An Unusual Throne

The essence of Jesus' parables in Luke 15 is this: His mercy flows abundantly, without barriers, to anyone inclined to receive it.

In the parable of the loving father, the elder brother stands outside the celebration, seething with resentment. To him, his younger brother is not a returning son but a banished outsider, one who brought chaos, waste, humiliation, and pain upon their family. As music and laughter fill the air, his fists clench. The dancing, the feasting—it all feels like a cruel and unjust joke. For years, he has done everything right. He has obeyed, followed the rules, and worked without complaint. And yet where is his party? Where is his reward (Luke 15:25–32)?

What he cannot see is that, in all his striving, he has become just as lost as his younger brother, only in a different way. His brother wandered in reckless rebellion; he is wandering in self-righteousness. Yet beneath his indignation lies something even deeper: self-interest. His true fear is not merely injustice, it is loss. With his brother's return, will his own share of the inheritance shrink? His mind, like his brother's before him, is fixed not on his father's love but on his father's eventual passing and the payday he expects to receive. In the end both sons have betrayed their father's heart.

But the father, who rightfully owns and stewards all of the family's wealth, is not focused on resources at all. His greatest treasures, despite their entitled and disrespectful treatment of him, are his two sons—the one who has come home and the one who never left. While he celebrates the return of the prodigal, the father tenderly reminds the elder son, "All I have is yours."

Jesus' stories are not just signposts, they are declarations of his rule. He is not just inviting the lost back home, he is reclaiming them as family. His mercy is not weakness, it is the very power by which he reigns.

And the cross of Jesus is his throne, the place where mercy and justice meet. It delivers two crucial messages: first, that we are lost beyond our ability to save ourselves; and second, that our King has made a way not by turning a blind eye to our sin but by bearing its weight himself. The cross stands as both diagnosis and cure, revealing the depth of our need and the even greater depth of his mercy.

Scripture also tells us we are surrounded by "a great cloud of witnesses," saints and angels cheering us on as we run our race, "looking to Jesus, the founder and perfecter of our faith, who for the joy that was set before him endured the cross, despising the shame" (Heb. 12:1–2 ESV). The "joy that was set before him" was not something he was missing; it was us—his lost and bleating sheep, his beloved children scattered in the wilderness of sin and doubt and fear, hesitant yet longing, deep down, to be led back home.

C. S. Lewis once wrote, "If I find in myself desires which nothing in this world can satisfy, the only logical explanation is that I was made for another world."[7] Our feelings of incompleteness and longing are reminders that we are made for more than this life as we know it. Even when we catch only glimpses of this deeper reality, Jesus' determined pursuit assures us that the joy of true and complete belonging will one day be ours. He will make sure of it.

Even on the cross, Jesus' final conversation was with a man the world considered beyond saving: one of the two thieves crucified alongside him. At first, this man joined his colleague in mocking Jesus. But something changed within him. In a moment of self-awareness and clarity, he turned to Jesus and asked, "Will you please remember me in your kingdom?" It is not a theologically refined request. It is not an eloquent prayer. It is the anguished cry of a dying man who knows he has nothing to offer, and that is enough.

The cross, meant to be a place of disgrace, is in reality a coronation. The world had its idea of kings—men of power, dominance, and wealth. But Jesus, the Mercy King, rules differently. His throne is a cross. His crown is woven with thorns. And his kingdom is populated by those the world calls unworthy, but whom he calls beloved. With the mocking sign above his head that says, "King of the Jews," Jesus declares with authority to the dying thief, "Truly, I say to you, today you will be with me in paradise" (Luke 23:42–43 ESV).

The Man on the Middle Cross

Pastor Alistair Begg offers a powerful reflection on this scene. He imagines an angel asking the thief upon his arrival in heaven, "How did that happen? You were cursing him out, never attended a Bible study, weren't baptized, and knew nothing about church membership. Yet here you are. How did you make it?" In Begg's retelling, the thief replies, "The man on the middle cross said I could come."[8]

This is the heart of grace. Martin Luther once said that most of Christianity is lived outside of us, not by us.[9] This means that all of our redemption was accomplished and applied by Christ himself. Our salvation is secured not by what our hands have done but through the life, death, burial, resurrection, and pursuing love of Christ alone. From the middle cross, his voice also calls out to us, "You too can come."

The middle cross declares that no one is too lost, broken, or far gone to be wanted and embraced by Jesus, the Mercy King. This invitation isn't limited to the past, it extends to us now. This very moment, we are invited to receive and find rest in this very same grace. The cross of Jesus, which reveals both our lostness without him and our belonging with him, stands as a beacon of hope.

It also stands as an invitation into community. If we have been accepted, how can we withhold acceptance? If we have been forgiven, how can we refuse to forgive? Jesus' mercy is not a limited gift to hoard, it is a multiplying gift to extend. Who in your life needs to experience his mercy from you? The coworker who frustrates you? The friend who hurt or betrayed you? The stranger whose life looks nothing like yours? Mercy is not just something we receive, it is given to be shared.

As we embrace the mercies of Christ, let us remember who he is: the Mercy King, who reigns with kindness and truth, justice and grace.

In his kingdom, there are no outcasts.

There are only those who are wanted, welcomed, and loved.

Summary

Human brokenness, guilt, and shame often convince us that we are beyond mercy, but Jesus, the Mercy King, proves otherwise. He does not wait for the lost to find their way back; he pursues them relentlessly. Through parables like those of the lost sheep, the lost coin, and the prodigal son, Jesus reveals a God who seeks, restores, and rejoices over those whom society (and even their own hearts) might label as out of reach. Our deepest failures and doubts do not push him away, they draw him closer. At the cross, he proves once and for all that his invitation is for everyone. The only question is, Will we come?

Three Questions

1. In what ways has guilt, shame, or self-doubt made you feel unworthy of God's love? How have these feelings shaped your view of yourself and your relationship with him?
2. Jesus pursues the lost not with reluctance but with joy. How does his pursuit, as seen in the parables of Luke 15, reshape your understanding of how he sees you, even at your worst?
3. Who in your life most needs to experience this same mercy? How can you, as someone who has been welcomed by Jesus, extend that welcome to them?

One Action Step

Think of an area of your life where shame, regret, or self-condemnation still linger. In prayer or journaling, name that burden honestly before Jesus. Then instead of rehearsing guilt, imagine yourself as a prodigal daughter or son returning home, only to be embraced before you can even finish your apology. Write down your hopes about what being fully wanted, fully received, and fully restored is like. Then describe that feeling based on what you now know about the King's mercy.

TWO

When Power Fails You

The Mercy King Who Redefines Greatness

> The great reversal—Jesus as servant, not master; as crucified, not crowned—redefines what it means to be human.
>
> —Eugene Peterson, *The Jesus Way*

From the beginning, human history has been driven by an obsession with greatness.

We love to win, hate to lose, and often believe that power and prestige are the keys to staying on top. But have you ever noticed that even when you achieve what you thought would satisfy, it still feels like something is missing? That success, recognition, wealth—even good things—leave a void that won't go away?

This impulse to matter shapes both individuals and entire societies. But has it delivered what it promised?

Our tragic human story begins in Eden, where Adam and Eve

chose independence over trust. Tempted by the serpent's promise that they could be like God, they reached not only for knowledge but for autonomy—a life on their own terms, apart from the protective, life-giving leadership of their Creator. It wasn't just disobedience, it was a coup attempt, a grasping for preeminence, a bid to be in charge. In seeking to take what belongs only to God, they lost the freedom they already had. Their decision set in motion a pattern of conflict and chaos that still defines the human experience.

That same pattern showed up at Babel, where humanity, united in pride, tried to reach heaven on their own and make a name for themselves. But their pursuit of greatness ended in confusion and scattering. Once again self-glorification led to fragmentation (Gen. 11:1–9).

We see it again in Babylon. King Nebuchadnezzar demanded worship and built a monument to his power, only to be brought low in humiliation. History continues to prove the point: When we seek to exalt ourselves, it always ends in a fall (Dan. 3:1–25).

Like Humpty-Dumpty, the world's prideful powers have always sat high, only to experience a great fall. And no matter how many kings' horses or men try to put them back together again, they can't. Kingdoms rise and kingdoms fall, one after the next.

Still we keep repeating the story. In modern life we build our worldviews around the same old ideas, just in new clothes. Science, politics, and cultural systems still tend to follow the same mantra: Only the strong survive. Darwin's theory of the survival of the fittest shapes more than biology; it also shapes how we see power, progress, and people. Friedrich Nietzsche went farther, claiming that the human will to power is central to our nature, and that greatness belongs to those strong enough to rise above the rest. His vision of the *Übermensch*, or "superman," portrayed strength, dominance, and self-rule as the highest goods. But the result was not freedom, it was fear and control.

This same hunger for greatness showed up in the Enlightenment, when human reason and ingenuity were seen as the solution to all of life's problems. The "Age of Reason" preached a message of limitless potential, with some imagining humanity as the new savior of the world. Poet Algernon Swinburne captured the spirit of the time in the line "Glory to man in the highest," as though we were on the verge of creating heaven on earth.[1]

That same spirit lived on into the twentieth century. In 1973 more than 150 secular scholars signed the *Humanist Manifesto*, declaring that human beings had mastered the planet. They claimed that technology could solve poverty, reshape human behavior, cure cancer and all infectious disease, even rewrite evolution itself. It was a vision of redemption, but without a redeemer.

Time and time again, we have been promised a better world: smarter systems, more progress, and greater control over our future. But here we are—more advanced, yet more anxious and lonelier than ever. Promising careers leave people empty. Politics continues to disappoint. If progress alone could save us, wouldn't we be saved by now?

The truth is, no leader, no political party, no merely human vision for a better world has ever fully delivered on its promises. Even our most sincere efforts fall short. We repeat the same cycles, chasing the same hopes, only to be met with the same disappointments.

And we're left asking why. What are we missing?

Into this tired, predictable cycle steps Jesus, the Mercy King. Unlike the many emperors and caesars, his kingdom is not built on domineering, self-promotion, or a curated public image. He secures power not by grasping for more but by giving himself away. He subverts every expectation of what a leader should be, offering instead a radically different vision of greatness, one grounded not in self-exaltation but in self-giving mercy.

Jesus is the King who stoops. Who descends to serve. Who

suffers for the sake of others. And in doing so, he reveals not just a better way to lead but a better way to live.

If this is how the true King lives, then maybe our relentless quest for greatness is the very thing that's keeping us from the life we were made for. History has shown us that human ambition—no matter how impressive—can't carry the weight of our deepest hopes. So where do we turn?

We turn to him.

The way of Jesus is counterintuitive, even unsettling at first. But it's also deeply freeing. What if the way up has always been down? What if laying down our need to prove ourselves is the first step toward flourishing? What if our chase for power and prestige has been a trap all along, and humble surrender is the way out?

The world urges us to climb higher. Jesus calls us to kneel. He says, "Whoever would be great among you must be your servant" (Mark 10:43 ESV). In his kingdom, greatness is found not in rising above others but in lowering ourselves in love.

Jesus, the Mercy King, doesn't follow the world's playbook for power or greatness. He turns it upside down. In this chapter, we'll look at why his way, though often unexpected, is the more excellent way.

The Mercy King Elevates the Lowly

There's a quiet, mysterious pattern woven into the way God works: Those the world sees as small or insignificant are often the very ones he calls, values, and lifts up. The apostle Paul speaks directly to this in his first letter to the Corinthians, a community known for chasing status, power, and prestige. Corinth was a city captivated by influence and upward mobility, always striving but never quite arriving.

Paul writes, "Brothers and sisters, think of what you were when you were called. Not many of you were wise by human standards; not many were influential; not many were of noble birth" (1 Cor. 1:26).

To the ears of Corinth's cultural elite—its movers and shakers—these words must have landed with force. Paul is essentially saying, "In a world obsessed with becoming somebody, most of you were nobodies." They hadn't risen through the ranks of society. They weren't powerful, wealthy, or regarded as wise by the world's standards. They weren't the ones people followed, they were the ones people overlooked.

And yet from that lowly place, God chose them.

If you've ever felt invisible or inadequate—if you've ever questioned whether you have the goods—you are in good company. You're the kind of person Jesus calls. He doesn't pay much attention to résumés, reputations, or social status. He looks at the heart. His kingdom is made up of the underqualified and the unlikely. Of people who sometimes feel like impostors, who carry the shame of losing, who wonder whether they'll ever get their break.

To all of them—and to all of us—Jesus says, "You are known. You are wanted. You are mine." In the kingdom of God, the forgotten are not forgotten. And the unworthy are made worthy—not by merit but by mercy.

In the world of the New Testament, lineage was everything. Your family tree served as your résumé, a testament to your status and significance in the world. It was not your individual achievements, talents, or hard work that mattered but the legacy handed down to you. Social elites would even edit their genealogies, removing unimpressive or embarrassing ancestors and bold printing those who bolstered their prestige. Their family name was their boast.

For those outside this culture of social climbing, life offered no stage. Without the right family connections, you were invisible within the social and professional hierarchy, disposable and often discarded. Yet Paul's message was directed at these overlooked individuals. While Corinthian society deemed them insignificant, in God's eyes, they were chosen. Their boast was not in noble bloodlines but in their identity as God's daughters and sons.

This pattern continues in the lives of Jesus' closest, chosen followers. They were ordinary women and men with flaws, fears, and failures. Among them were tax collectors, despised for their collaboration with Rome; zealots with violent inclinations; doubters and skeptics; and a few prostitutes. Peter swore loyalty to Jesus only to deny him three times when it mattered most. Thomas refused to believe in the resurrection until he touched Jesus' wounds. These were not the religious elite or the morally upright; they were the ones Jesus referred to as "you of little faith." And still they were his chosen, because weakness is the vessel through which the Mercy King does his best work. By worldly measures, none of Jesus' disciples were destined for greatness. And yet it was their lack of worldly significance that made them the perfect instruments for his agenda.

If you've ever felt small, take heart: You are exactly the kind of person the Mercy King receives and deploys. His kingdom isn't about prestige or power. It is given to the poor in spirit, the meek, and those who hunger and thirst for a righteousness they can't attain on their own. Jesus builds his family tree not with the impressive but with the imperfect. His rule is not for those who have it all together but for those who come with empty hands and receptive hearts.

Paul continues, "God chose what is foolish in the world to shame the wise . . . what is low and despised . . . so that no human being might boast" (1 Cor. 27–29 ESV). With these words, he exposes a universal idol that Corinth cherishes, but did not invent: the fixation on status and being connected to influential people. Paul isn't condemning power and position themselves but the pride, self-importance, and craving for recognition that often accompany them. God can and certainly does use people in high positions for his work, but when worldly pride and self-importance supplant the spirit of humble service, we step into dangerous territory.

When we start viewing ourselves as choice rather than chosen, we miss the point.

Paul's challenge to the Corinthians is relevant today, especially in societies like ours. Take my own city of Nashville, where social status and connections function as a kind of unspoken currency. The tendency to name-drop or seek validation through proximity to celebrities, influencers, and gatekeepers reveals the motivations of the heart. It's easy to spot when someone starts cozying up to people who can boost their status, while quietly pulling away from those with less influence or power. But it can be harder to spot when we're doing it ourselves.

Nashville is not unique in this. Paul's message could apply to any of us. Don't we all make subtle calculations about who is worth our time? Who do we choose to welcome into our lives? How many of our friends sit above us on our self-imposed social ladder, and how many are below? Who do we invite into our homes and share meals with, and who gets left out? A life built around status and exclusivity may seem appealing, but ultimately it reveals itself as an empty dead-end street.

Twentieth-century minister Martyn Lloyd-Jones offers a different vision of greatness. Before becoming a preacher, he was a distinguished physician, moving easily within elite circles. But Lloyd-Jones felt called to pastoral ministry and found deeper kinship among the working-class people he served in a Welsh mining town. Later he reflected that this bond, formed with people of modest means and no societal standing, was stronger than any he'd once had with the educated, high-status elites who did not share his faith.

C. S. Lewis presents a similar vision in *The Great Divorce*, where he introduces Sarah Smith, an ordinary woman whose quiet, humble life seemed inconsequential in the world's eyes. Yet in heaven, she is treated as a person of immense honor, surrounded by those whose lives were touched by her quiet, faithful acts of love and kindness.[2] Sarah Smith's story echoes Lloyd-Jones' insight about the humble townspeople—faithful, unpretentious souls who lacked worldly status but shared a meaningful connection with God and each other. As Jesus famously said, "Blessed are the meek, for they will inherit the earth" (Matt. 5:5).

These examples remind us that God often lifts up those the world overlooks. He values loyalty, kindness, and humility far more than fame, credentials, or status. This reversal of values—where the last become first and the humble are exalted—though lovely, can also be unsettling. It confronts our assumptions, especially in the places we hold most dear.

One of those places is parenting.

If you are a parent—or hope to be—consider the dreams you carry for your children. When you picture their future, what do you want for them most? Do you imagine them marrying someone successful and well connected, even if their faith is weak or absent? Or if you had to choose, would you rather they build a life with someone of humble means and moderate worldly ambition, but with a deep, authentic relationship with Jesus?

What do we count as negotiable? And what, in our hearts, do we treat as nonnegotiable? These are searching questions meant not to shame but to reveal. They help us uncover what we truly value.

What are we preparing our children for? Are we pointing them chiefly toward prestigious schools, high-paying jobs, and elite social circles without also grounding them in the deeper, lasting treasures of faith, integrity, community, and service? Are we subtly guiding them toward the very kind of status-seeking Paul warned the Corinthians to leave behind?

Wanting our children to succeed is good and natural. But if we're not careful, we can unknowingly lead them—and ourselves—into a version of success that is distanced from the Mercy King's heart.

The world rewards prominence. Jesus blesses the pure in heart. And in the long run, it is the latter who win at life.

The Mercy King Humbles the Proud

At the heart of God's kingdom lies a striking paradox: Those considered to be small by the world are often great in God's eyes, and those considered to be great are brought low. This reversal is meant not to shame the powerful or successful but to offer real hope, even to those who have much. Jesus himself pointed to this paradox when he said it's harder for the rich to enter the kingdom of God than for a camel to pass through the eye of a needle. And yet he immediately followed with reassurance: "With man it is impossible, but not with God. For all things are possible with God" (Mark 10:17–27 ESV).

The apostle Paul knew this paradox intimately. Once a rising star within religious circles, Paul had the education, pedigree, and drive to secure a seat among the elite. In Philippians he recalls how he outpaced his peers as a young rabbi. But looking back, he calls all those achievements "rubbish"—a softened translation of a much stronger term—compared with the surpassing worth of knowing Christ (Phil. 3:8 ESV). For Paul, building an identity on worldly success was ultimately hollow. It all fades. In the end, it's just us and God.

On that final day, we'll echo Job's words: "Naked I came from my mother's womb, and naked I shall return." Can we also say, with Job, "The Lord gave, and the Lord has taken away; blessed be the name of the Lord" (Job 1:21 ESV)? That's Paul's challenge. And his invitation.

This perspective shaped how Paul viewed status and influence in the church as well. In Corinth he noticed a growing culture of personality, where believers began aligning themselves with favorite leaders: "I follow Paul," "I follow Peter," "I follow Apollos." It was the first-century version of a preacher fan club, where spiritual authority became tangled up with personal loyalty and popularity.

Paul responded not with flattery but with clarity: "What is Paul? What is Apollos? Servants. Only God gives the growth." (See 1 Cor. 3:5–6.) For Paul, preaching was never about gathering a personal following or building a brand. It was always about pointing people to Jesus. If Christ wasn't at the center, Paul would have said, keep looking. Find someone who leads you to him.

This theme—God's delight in humble, godward people—runs throughout Scripture. We see it in the Roman centurion who came to Jesus, pleading for healing on behalf of his servant. Though powerful and respected, the centurion showed compassion toward someone far beneath him in status—a rare trait in a world that often discards the weak.

When Jesus offered to come and heal the servant, the centurion replied with stunning humility, "I am not worthy to have you come under my roof, but only say the word, and my servant will be healed" (Matt. 8:8–9 ESV). Jesus marveled at this man's faith. Here was a Roman commander bowing before a poor, wandering rabbi. The centurion knew that true authority didn't rest with Caesar, it rested with Jesus. And true greatness, he understood, is not about climbing higher but about bowing lower.

As late pastor and seminary professor Jack Miller often said, "Grace flows downhill." God's grace tends to meet us when we stop trying to prove ourselves and instead open our hands in surrender. It's only then that his blessing has room to come in.

This is the same truth Jesus declared in the Sermon on the Mount, in which he lifted up those the world overlooks. The poor in spirit. The meek. The mourning. These, he said, are the true heirs of the kingdom. If we asked Jesus where celebrity resides in his kingdom, he wouldn't point to the famous, he would point to the invisible. To the overlooked. To someone like Sarah Smith.

One of the deepest joys in my pastoral life has been watching how the humble are honored in church communities. In one congregation I served, individuals with special needs became our in-house "celebrities." They were cherished and celebrated, not out of pity but out of a genuine recognition that in God's kingdom, they model what greatness looks like.

Henri Nouwen experienced something similar. A former professor at Notre Dame, Yale, and Harvard, Nouwen left the world of academic elites to live among those with intellectual and developmental disabilities at Daybreak, a L'Arche community in Canada. At first he thought he was there to serve. But in time he realized he was there to be served—by people the world often overlooks.

Reflecting on his experience, Nouwen writes, "If people with special needs express love for you, it comes from God. It's not because of your accomplishments or fame. They love because it's a gift." This realization led Nouwen to proclaim that these so-called "broken, wounded, and completely unpretentious" individuals helped him shed the part of himself that was always trying to impress and achieve. In their presence he learned to let go of the relevant self and embrace the vulnerable self— the self that simply loves and is loved.[3]

So how might this apply to us?

As you go through your week, consider the names below yours on the organizational chart. When dining out, take notice of the person refilling your water or clearing your table. If you pass someone asking for help on the street, pause. You may be looking at future royalty in God's kingdom. You may be encountering the next Sarah Smith.

As pastor and theologian Francis Schaeffer once said, "There are no little people."[4]

All of this comes into full view in the life, death, and resurrection of Jesus, the Mercy King, who made himself nothing for our sakes. He is not distant from our weakness; he entered into it. He was tempted in every way, just as we are, yet without sin (Heb. 4:15). His descent into suffering and humility—what the world saw as defeat—was, in the eyes of heaven, his great victory.

Ironically, and beautifully, what the world called losing was the very definition of winning.

The King Who Made Himself Nothing

Paul draws us to the very center of his message with these words: "The word of the cross is folly to those who are perishing, but to us who are being saved it is the power of God" (1 Cor. 1:18 ESV).

At the cross, the kingdom of God collided with the world's version of power, a world where rulers demand loyalty, enforce their will through coercion, and maintain control by fear. By those standards, the cross looked like weakness: a failed Messiah, rejected, humiliated, and crucified. But Jesus' kingly triumph is not of this world. He does not crush his enemies, he dies for them. He doesn't demand tribute, he becomes the ransom. His kingship is built not through conquest but through mercy. And through this mercy, he reigns forever.

In Jesus, mercy is not weakness. It's not passivity. It is power—power of the highest kind. A kind that topples empires not through domination but through love. For those who belong to Christ, the cross is not foolish. It is the clearest expression of God's might and grace.

A scene from *Jesus Christ Superstar* captures this tension

between worldly strength and divine humility. Pilate, bewildered and condescending, looks at Jesus and asks, "Who is this broken man cluttering up my hall? Who is this unfortunate?"

A soldier replies, "King of the Jews."

Surprised, Pilate responds, "So this is Jesus Christ? I'm really quite surprised. You look so small—not a king at all."[5]

Pilate could see only weakness. He didn't realize that the broken man standing before him was the true governor and king, whose reign would outlast Caesar's and whose kingdom would never end. Pilate saw a man to be dismissed. He missed the truth: that this man would rise from the dead and usher in a new way of being human where greatness is defined not by raw power but by humble service.

Jesus' strength wasn't in resisting suffering, it was in choosing it. He laid down his life not only for the victim but also for the villain. For those who have been harmed, and for those who have done harm. For those trying to climb the ladder, and for those crushed beneath it.

That is true power.

Imagine the strength it takes for the all-powerful, sinless Son of God to endure rejection, torture, and death, knowing he could have stopped it all with a single word. Yet he didn't. As Paul writes, "Though he was in the form of God, he did not count equality with God a thing to be grasped, but emptied himself . . . becoming obedient to the point of death, even death on a cross" (Phil. 2:6–8 ESV).

And because of that humility, because of that descent, Scripture tells us that one day "every knee should bow . . . and every tongue confess that Jesus Christ is Lord" (vv. 10–11 ESV).

God's grace collects not in the high places of pride or performance but in the low places of surrender. God opposes the proud but gives grace to the humble. This is the vision James echoes when he calls the rich and powerful to take pride not in their status but in their low position in Christ (James 1:9–10). Because in God's economy, the true boast is this:

Apart from Christ, I can do nothing.

Apart from Christ, I am weak, mortal, and needy.

Apart from Christ, I am, in truth, very small, not a king at all.

But in Christ—with all his beloved and lowly ones—I will inherit the earth.

Paul Tripp captures this upside-down vision of grace so well: "In Christ, death is the doorway to life. Hopelessness is the entrance to hope. Weakness is the place to find strength. . . . Defeat is actually a victory. The end is really a beginning. . . . Hope is sung to suffering's tune. Life is played on death's instruments. Grace doesn't play by the law's score. God composes hope from tragedy's notes."[6]

Jesus, the Mercy King, welcomes every type of person into his kingdom: the CEO and the janitor, the well known and the overlooked, the wise and the wondering, the strong and the struggling. His invitation is not reserved for the religious elite or the morally impressive. It is wide open for anyone ready to come with empty hands and a willing heart.

This isn't just a general invitation, it's a personal one. Jesus isn't just calling people, he's calling you. Right where you are. With all your doubts, all your failures, all your fear. You don't have to prove anything. You don't need to earn your place. The table is already set. Your seat is already reserved. The price has already been paid. To you, Jesus says, "Come."

In the end, you will be judged or measured not by your performance or status but by your union with and belonging to Jesus Christ. As my close friend Rankin Wilbourne has said, "God does not love you to the degree that you are like Christ. Rather, he loves you to the degree that you are *in* Christ, and that's one hundred percent."

From that secure place, he invites you to participate in a kingdom where greatness looks like servanthood, where thrones are traded for towels, and where crowns are made of thorns. His is the kingdom of grace. The rule of the Mercy King.

Your seat is ready. Your place is secure. The only question is, Are you ready to take your rightful place?

Summary

From Eden to today, the human heart has been shaped by the ache to matter—to prove itself through status, strength, and success. But again and again Scripture and history reveal the same pattern: self-exaltation leads to collapse, while humble surrender leads to life. In Jesus, the Mercy King, we see a better way. He redefines greatness not by ascending to power but by descending in love. He chose the cross over a throne, servanthood over status, and humility over acclaim. His kingdom is upside down, but it's also right side up. In his rule, the weak are welcomed, the overlooked are honored, and the proud are invited to step down into grace. True significance isn't something we earn, it's something we receive. And the good news is, your place in his kingdom is already prepared.

Three Questions

1. Where do you see the hunger for power, recognition, or relevance show up in your own life, and what lies beneath it?
2. How does Jesus' example of humility and self-giving love reshape your understanding of greatness, leadership, or influence?
3. Who in your life might be overlooked, undervalued, or unseen, and how can you honor them the way Jesus would?

One Action Step

For the next thirty days, post this truth somewhere you'll see it often—on your mirror, desk, dashboard, or phone lock screen. Let it recenter your heart each day: "My value is found not in what I achieve but in the one who gave himself for me. I am defined not by how high I climb but by how deeply I am loved."

Let this reminder shape how you see yourself—and everyone around you—as people beloved by the Mercy King.

THREE

When Your Heart Has Been Hijacked

The Mercy King Who Breaks the Grip of Lesser Gods

> Idolatry is not just a failure to obey God, it is a setting of the whole heart on something besides God. This cannot be remedied only by repenting that you have an idol, or using willpower to try to live differently. Turning from idols is not less than those two things, but it is also far more. Setting the mind and heart on things above means appreciating, rejoicing, and resting in what Jesus has done for you.
>
> —Timothy Keller, *Counterfeit Gods*

At the very core of who we are, we are worshipers.

Whether or not we realize it, our hearts are always offering devotion to someone or something. John Calvin once wrote, "Man's nature, so to speak, is a perpetual factory of idols."[1] Put another way, we are continually crafting substitutes for the God who made us. His observation reveals a sobering truth: When God is not at the center of our affection and trust, something else inevitably takes his place. And yet we were created for one great purpose: to know, love, and worship God alone.

Beneath every longing we carry—every ache for beauty, meaning, or connection—is a deeper, more primal desire: a yearning for our Creator. As the apostle Paul writes in Romans, "For from him and through him and for him are all things" (Rom. 11:36). Everything begins and ends with him.

This is why idolatry is far more than just a moral misstep. It is a rupture in relationship. It is our hearts seeking life in what cannot give it. And yet into our restless idol-chasing, Jesus enters—not as a scolding judge but as the Mercy King. He comes not to shame us but to shepherd us home. He exposes and confronts the futility of our false gods not to condemn us but to lead us back to the only one worthy of our worship: himself.

He does this not with the force of a sword but with the tender strength of his scars. His rule is built not on domination but on deliverance. This is the beauty of his kingship: He reigns by redeeming, not by crushing. When we wander, he doesn't discard us. He restores us. He reorients us toward the wisdom of St. Augustine's prayer, "You have made us for yourself, O Lord, and our heart is restless until it rests in you."[2]

From the very beginning, idolatry has marked the human story. In ancient times, people bowed before carved images of stone or wood. Today our idols may wear different disguises, but their power is just as real. Careers, relationships, achievements, or material wealth can quietly rise to take the throne of our hearts. Idolatry takes hold anytime we entrust our deepest hopes, identity, or sense of worth to anything—or anyone—other than God.

What Is Idolatry? And Why Only a Mercy King Can Defeat It

Idolatry, at its heart, is giving something—or someone—a place in our lives that belongs to God alone. When he says to us, "You shall have no other gods before me" (Ex. 20:3), he is not asking to be first in a lineup of priorities; he is inviting us to live with him as our one and only.

This isn't because God is needy or threatened by competition. Far from it. His demand for exclusivity is born of love, not insecurity. As C. S. Lewis once observed, "God made us: invented us as a man invents an engine. A car is made to run on petrol, and it would not run properly on anything else. Now God designed the human machine to run on himself."[3] We weren't created to run on applause, ambition, relationships, or riches. We were made to run on God.

And yet how often we try to fuel our lives with lesser things. The result is always the same: breakdown, confusion, disappointment. Still, the King who made us for himself does not recoil from our messes. He moves toward us. Not with folded arms and furrowed brows but with nail-scarred hands and mercy in his eyes. Jesus, the Mercy King, steps into our disordered loves and misaligned loyalties not to condemn but to rescue. "You shall have no other gods before me" is not a threat. It is an invitation. It is the wooing voice of the one who alone can satisfy the ache we keep trying to soothe with counterfeits. His glory and our good are not at odds; they are wonderfully aligned.

The first commandment was radically countercultural when first spoken. After four hundred years in Egypt—where gods were assigned to the sun, the Nile, and even the Pharaoh—the Israelites had soaked in a worldview in which divinity was everywhere and in everything. So when Yahweh declared himself to be the only true God, it was revolutionary. Yet even after witnessing God's power in their deliverance, the people still longed for something tangible, predictable, and controllable. In the wilderness, they crafted a golden calf—a toxic blend of their craving for money and power (Exodus 32). They wanted a god they could see, manage, and define. But the irony, then and now, is this: When we try to control our gods, they end up controlling us.

Though we may not bow before statues today, the impulse hasn't changed. As Origen once said, "What each one honors before all else, what before all things he adores and loves, this for him is his god."[4] Our modern idols may not look like golden calves or carved images, but they are no less present—or powerful. The human heart, as much as ever, remains susceptible to give ultimate devotion to things that were never meant to carry that kind of weight.

For some, the idol is comfort. We organize our lives around ease, convenience, and the absence of discomfort. We may not say it out loud, but often our greatest annoyance is being inconvenienced or disrupted. When comfort becomes ultimate, anything that challenges our peace feels like a threat, be it a hard conversation, a needy neighbor, or a call to sacrifice.

For others the idol is control. We find our sense of security in having a tight grip on our schedules, our children's futures, or the five-year plan we've mapped out in our minds. But when life inevitably veers off script—and it always does—we spiral into anxiety or anger because the thing we worship has failed us.

Still others may idolize reputation. We bend over backward to keep people impressed, afraid of letting others down or being misunderstood. We pour energy into maintaining a certain image—whether as the capable parent, the wise leader, the steady friend—believing our value is bound up in how we are perceived. But this kind of living chips away at the soul. The pursuit of image becomes a treadmill: No matter how fast we run, we never quite arrive.

These are just a few of the gospels of our age: comfort, control, approval. But they are gospels that cannot save. They promise peace, identity, and worth, but in the end, they don't deliver. Because only Christ can tell us who we are. Only Christ can give us the safety, the love, and the meaning our hearts crave. And unlike the idols we chase, he doesn't demand that we keep proving ourselves worthy of him; he invites us to rest in his finished work.

At its root, idolatry is self-deception. It's the liar and deceiver within whispering, "God isn't enough. You need more." But idols always promise more than they can deliver. They stir longing but never satisfy it. From Eden onward, this has been the pattern. Adam and Eve believed the lie that they could become like God if only they seized autonomy. And in the end, the knowledge they gained did not empower them. It shattered them.

Idolatry doesn't just disappoint. It enslaves. It speaks with a sweet voice but tightens its grip the more we reach for it. We check our accounts for peace, our phones for significance, our titles and salaries for identity. But still, we're restless. We tell ourselves we're in control, but deep down we sense the truth: We are being handled by the very things we thought we could handle.

Even when we see the truth about our idols, breaking free can feel impossible. Idols don't just shape our behavior, they shape our wants and identities. And this is why we need more than discipline or willpower. We need deliverance. We need someone stronger. The grip of idolatry may be fierce, but there is one whose grip is stronger still. A Mercy King who does not merely reveal the emptiness of our false gods, he conquers them. On the cross, Jesus did not simply unmask idolatry, he disarmed it. As Genesis 3:15 foretold, the serpent has been crushed beneath the feet of the risen King. Sin and death have been defeated. Our idols, once enthroned in our lives, have lost their claim—not because we tried harder but because Jesus triumphed on our behalf.

Idols that once enslaved us no longer have the right to rule, because our freedom has been purchased not with silver or gold but with the blood of the Mercy King.

How Idolatry Starts

Idolatry rarely announces itself with loud rebellion. More often, it begins quietly—through subtle shifts in our thoughts, priorities, and choices. Like addiction, it unfolds slowly. One small compromise leads to another, and over time the cumulative effect pulls us farther from the God who made us. It's like the proverbial frog in a pot of slowly boiling water, unaware of the danger until it's too late.

The apostle Paul offers clarity in Romans 1:18–19: "The wrath of God is being revealed from heaven against all the godlessness and wickedness of people, who suppress the truth by their wickedness, since what may be known about God is plain to them, because God has made it plain to them."

To understand this sobering passage, we must first understand the nature of God's wrath. It is not impulsive, unpredictable, or cruel, as human anger so often is. Rather it is holy, deliberate, and just. God's wrath is an expression of his deep love, a form of moral opposition to what harms us. God is like a skilled physician who refuses to tolerate a spreading cancer: His anger toward sin is rooted in his commitment to heal and restore. When God "gives people over" to their desires, it is not because he is indifferent but because he honors our agency. It's as if he says, "Even though it breaks my heart, I will let you go your own way." This form of passive wrath is not about exacting punishment but about letting us experience the natural consequences of our choices. And sometimes it is this kind of pain that wakes us up to our need for something better—*someone* better.

God does not desire coerced obedience; he longs for willing, trusting sons and daughters. His wrath, even in its severity, is measured and purposeful. Yet rather than respond with repentance, we often suppress the truth we already know. Sometimes this suppression comes from the desire to remain in control. At other times it stems from a kind of intellectual dishonesty—a refusal to acknowledge what is plain about God because doing so would require surrender.

In this sense, idolatry is a form of self-sabotage. We trade wisdom for foolishness and truth for a numbing illusion. Theologian David Wells put it bluntly: "Worldliness is whatever makes sin look normal and righteousness look strange."[5]

Even atheism is not free from the need for faith. Sir Fred Hoyle, the famed British astronomer and no friend to religious belief, once admitted that the odds of life originating by chance were as unlikely as a tornado assembling a Boeing 747 from a junkyard.[6] And yet like many others, he chose to believe in randomness over a creator. Belief in a godless universe requires its own leap, one that many are still willing to take.

But idolatry doesn't usually begin with outright denial of God's existence. More often it begins with a quiet resistance to the truth of Scripture. As 2 Timothy 3:16 reminds us, "All Scripture is God-breathed and is useful for teaching, rebuking, correcting and training in righteousness." When idolatry creeps in, we start to elevate our opinions, experiences, and preferences above the authority of God's Word. We embrace mantras like "follow your heart," "live your truth," or "let your conscience be your guide"—phrases that sound wise but subtly dethrone God as the one true guide for life.

The book of Judges gives us a haunting picture of what happens when truth is replaced by individual preference and impulse: "In those days there was no king in Israel. Everyone did what was right in his own eyes" (Judg. 17:6 ESV). Proverbs echoes this with a solemn warning: "There is a way that appears to be right, but in the end it leads to death" (Prov. 14:12).

This is the tragedy of idolatry: It's not just misguided affection, it's a fundamental exchange. David Foster Wallace, in his 2005 commencement speech at Kenyon College, captured this dynamic with alarming clarity:

> In the day-to-day trenches of adult life there is actually no such thing as atheism. There is no such thing as not worshiping. Everybody worships. The only choice we get is what to worship. And the compelling reason for maybe choosing some sort of God or spiritual-type thing to worship—be it J.C. or Allah, YHWH or the Wiccan Mother Goddess, or Zeus—you get the idea . . . is that pretty much anything else you worship will eat you alive. Worship money and things, if they are where you tap real meaning in life, then you will never have enough. Worship your body and beauty and sexual allure and you will always feel ugly. And when time and age start showing, you will die a million deaths before they finally grieve you. The whole trick is keeping the truth up front in daily consciousness.[7]

Idolatry is always a tragic exchange: the truth, beauty, and life found in God and his Word traded for illusions that cannot keep their promises. Like the Israelites in the wilderness, we often misplace our trust, only to find ourselves farther from the life we were created to live.

What we hope will heal us ends up haunting us.

Where We Are Most Susceptible to Idolatry

If you find yourself weary from chasing things that never seem to satisfy—if you've felt the hollow ache that follows the worship and service of anyone or anything that is not God—take heart. You are not beyond Christ's mercy. The very idols you struggle to let go of are the ones he came to overthrow. He doesn't shame those who return to him, he welcomes them. He lifts. He restores. And the battle you feel burdened to fight? He has already fought it for you.

Idolatry often finds its way into the places where we feel most insecure, vulnerable, or afraid. It preys on our longing for love, for worth, for stability. But the question isn't whether we will love or desire—because as human beings, we inevitably will. The more pressing question is what—or whom—we will love and desire most.

Augustine's idea of the "ordering of loves" speaks directly to this. When God holds the highest place in the hierarchy of our affections, everything else falls into its proper place. Paradoxically, when we fear God above all, we find we have nothing to be afraid of—not even him. It is the turning away from him, not the turning toward him, that leaves us most exposed.

Identifying the idols that quietly take root in our hearts requires honesty before God and with ourselves. This work of self-examination is not meant to shame but is meant to invite us into greater freedom and wholeness.

Ask yourself:

1. What do I believe I must have to be happy?
2. What creates anxiety or fear in me whenever it feels threatened, uncertain, or out of my control?
3. Where do my time, energy, and resources naturally flow without resistance?
4. In what areas am I tempted to ignore, adjust, or reinterpret Scripture to align with my desires?

These questions are not tests to pass but invitations to listen—to pay attention to what our hearts may be clinging to.

Beneath every false god is a longing for something good. And beneath every longing is the voice of the Mercy King wooing us, calling us back to himself.

Idolatry always disguises itself as something good, something we're meant to enjoy, but it quietly demands more than it should. It asks for what only God is entitled to.

One of Scripture's most poignant pictures of this slow drift is found in the life of King Solomon (1 Kings 11). Gifted with wisdom, wealth, and favor, Solomon had every reason to remain faithful. But over time his heart grew divided. Power, prestige, and the lure of many wives and concubines drew him away from single-hearted devotion. He began to build altars to foreign gods—chasing influence, security, and the illusion of happiness. But instead of flourishing, his soul fractured. The kingdom he had built with God's blessing began to unravel.

Solomon's story is sobering not because of some scandalous rebellion but because of how ordinary it feels. His downfall didn't happen in a moment. It came through a series of small compromises. Priorities shifted. Affections blurred. Convictions softened. And little by little, he wandered.

That same quiet drift shows up in our desire to be liked and included. We tell ourselves that if we can earn the approval of others—if we're agreeable enough, impressive enough, or easy enough to be around—the ache inside will finally subside. So we adapt. We edit ourselves. We silence convictions, soften our edges, and present only the parts of us we think will be accepted.

But even when others embrace us, something inside us can still feel off. Because over time we lose touch with the unique, "fearfully and wonderfully made" individuals God made us to be. The counterfeit sense of belonging we're chasing gets buried beneath a growing sense of disconnection from our true selves. In seeking to belong, we may find ourselves lonelier than before—not because others have dismissed or belittled us but because we've quietly started to dismiss and belittle ourselves.

Brené Brown once said, "Fitting in is about assessing a situation and becoming who you need to be to be accepted. Belonging, on the other hand, doesn't require us to change who we are; it requires us to be who we are."[8] But idolatry flips that script. It convinces us that changing, compromising, or performing is the necessary price of acceptance. And in the end, it offers connection but delivers loneliness.

Like the serpent in Eden, idolatry attaches itself to something good—a longing for love, meaning, or community—and quietly poisons it. It drains what was meant to be a gift and leaves us chasing shadows. It always promises more than it can give. And it always leaves us wanting.

The Impact of Idolatry

Idolatry, once rooted, inflicts harm on both individuals and communities. Elevating created things above the Creator leads to spiritual disorientation and profound misery.

Idolatry also distorts our identity. When we replace God with anything else, we lose sight of who we are as his image-bearers. The first of the Ten Commandments reflects God's design for human flourishing. Living according to his will brings wholeness, but when we turn to idols, we dishonor God and harm ourselves. Idolatry is like a fish taken out of water. Just as a fish cannot survive outside its natural habitat, we cannot thrive outside God's will. We become like fish gasping on dry land: restless, suffocating, and slowly dying. While idolatry may offer temporary pleasure, it accelerates our spiritual decay, much like savoring and swallowing a sweet but poisonous berry.

King Solomon's life is offered to us as a warning. Despite Solomon's being the wisest man who ever lived, his heart was drawn away by his desire not for a woman in particular but for women in general, as demonstrated by his harem of a thousand wives and concubines. He even constructed temples for the gods of his foreign wives, trading his devotion to the God of Abraham, Isaac, Jacob, and his father, David, to serve his insatiable libido. This divided loyalty led to the eventual downfall of his kingdom, serving as a sobering caution: Even the most gifted among us are susceptible to the lure of idolatry.

Idolatry's impact extends beyond the individual to entire communities. When families, organizations, or societies prioritize power, fame, or wealth over virtues like justice, mercy, and humility, decay becomes inevitable. People begin to view one another as competitors or tools for personal gain rather than as fellow image-bearers of God. This shift fosters division, exploitation, and confusion.

Politics is another realm where idolatry can cause catastrophic relational and societal harm. When political power becomes an idol, leaders may prioritize their agendas over the well-being of the people they serve. History is full of rulers who oppressed their citizens to maintain lordship. When the pursuit of power eclipses God's call for justice, mercy, and faithfulness, the fallout can be devastating not just for individuals but for entire nations.

The promises that idols make are enticing, but ultimately empty. Idolatry leaves us spiritually starved and relationally isolated. What promises satisfaction brings only greater emptiness.

In the end, idols don't just disappoint. They destroy.

How Idolatry Dies

Idolatry doesn't have to hold us captive forever. The grip it has on our hearts, habits, and hopes can be broken—not through striving but through a quiet, deliberate, ongoing exchange: replacing what is false with what is true.

Paul speaks directly into this process in Philippians 4:8, where he writes, "Whatever is true, whatever is noble, whatever is right, whatever is pure, whatever is lovely, whatever is admirable—if anything is excellent or praiseworthy—think about such things." Elsewhere, he calls it the renewal of our minds: "Do not conform to the pattern of this world, but be transformed by the renewing of your mind" (Rom. 12:2).

Orienting our thoughts toward God and his truth is the first and essential defense against the lies that threaten to take root in us. But this is not a passive posture. It requires intentionality: focused attention, quiet persistence, and often spiritual battle. Paul describes this dynamic in 2 Corinthians 10:5: "We demolish arguments and every pretension that sets itself up against the knowledge of God, and we take captive every thought to make it obedient to Christ."

These arguments and pretensions are subtle and persistent. They rarely sound evil; more often they sound almost right. But anything that seeks to replace God's voice with a lesser one must be confronted and replaced with the truth found in his Word.

I remember a season during graduate school when worry consumed my inner life. Anxieties about my health, my future, and whether my life would be meaningful took up most of my mental and emotional space. During that time, a wise and compassionate mentor shared a simple but transformative insight with me: "When intrusive thoughts come, you must talk to yourself more than you listen to yourself."

That sentence became a lifeline. Slowly it became a daily—sometimes minute by minute—practice. Rather than simply allowing my anxious thoughts to narrate my story, I spoke back to them, grounding my words in Scripture. Philippians 1:21 became a kind of anchor: "For to me, to live is Christ and to die is gain."

What I began to see was this: My fear of dying young wasn't just about mortality; it was rooted in a false belief that my life would be incomplete without certain accomplishments, milestones, or moments. But as I rehearsed God's truth to my soul, I was reminded that even Jesus—the most complete and impactful person who ever lived—walked the earth for only a little more than thirty years. And he did so with his eyes on "the joy set before him"—a joy that would not be fully realized until he returned to the Father in glory (Heb. 12:2).

That truth reoriented me. It reshaped how I viewed both life and death. I found myself drawn to the promises of Scripture that remind us that no matter how beautiful life becomes here, our best days are still ahead. Revelation 21 tells us that in the new heaven and new earth, our King will "'wipe every tear from [our] eyes. There will be no more death' or mourning or crying or pain, for the old order of things [will have] passed away," and everything will be made new (Rev. 21:4–5). Paul echoes this in 2 Corinthians 5:1, assuring us that when this "earthly tent" of ours fades away, we have awaiting us "a building from God, an eternal house in heaven."

This is how idolatry loses its power: when we allow God's truth to lovingly dismantle the lies we've been living by. It's also an act of surrender, a humble acknowledgment that only God has the right to define our lives and write our stories.

For me much of my struggle with idolatry came down to control. I wanted to hold the pen. Deep down I wasn't sure I could trust God to author my story well. But slowly, and with more faltering steps than I care to admit, I've been learning to hold my dreams, relationships, reputation, and ambitions with open hands. In that openness, I've discovered a kind of freedom that control could never offer.

Jesus has done for us what no idol ever could. On the cross, he didn't simply pay the penalty for our sin, he shattered sin's power.

The idols that once claimed authority over our lives no longer have the right to rule. The Mercy King has paid our ransom in full.

Letting go, then, isn't just an act of faith.

It's the doorway to peace.

It's the pathway to fullness.

It's how we begin to live free.

Jesus Is the Answer

Even when our faith falters, Jesus remains unwavering. He does not recoil from those who stumble, he draws near with compassion. The very idols we wrestle to release are the ones he gave his life to free us from. His mercy is not reserved for the spiritually strong, it is extended to the weak and faltering. He is not only the King we worship but also the Savior who bends low to lift us when we fall.

And even when we return to the very idols we once walked away from—"As a dog returns to its vomit, so fools repeat their folly" (Prov. 26:11)—even when we return to the things that will never love us back, his mercy remains and his love awaits our return.

There is only one thing in this world that cannot be lost: Jesus Christ, the Mercy King. Jobs come and go. Relationships change. Health falters. Success fades. Our lives are but a breath (Job 7:7). But through it all, Christ remains—unmoved, unchanging, and endlessly faithful. This is why the first commandment—"You shall have no other gods before me"—is an invitation. It calls us away from what cannot hold us, into the arms of the one who always will.

Unlike idols that demand and deplete, Jesus reigns and rescues. He is not merely a better alternative to false gods, he is the rightful King who alone deserves our total trust. His rule is marked by tenderness, yet his authority is absolute. To turn from idols is not just to reject deception; it is to make our way back home. It is to bow before the only one whose power is matched by his mercy.

No idol can do for us what Jesus has already done:

Idols demand our sacrifices; Jesus became the sacrifice.

Idols punish failure; Jesus forgives us in our failure.

Idols take life; Jesus gives it back, full and eternal.

He alone is worthy. He alone endures.

Idolatry is the greatest threat to human flourishing. It distorts our relationship with God, with ourselves, and with the world around us. It promises fulfillment but leaves us empty. It offers power but makes us slaves. Yet even when we fall into its grip, there is hope.

Jonah's story reminds us of this. After running from God and sinking into the depths of his rebellion, he cried out from the belly of a great fish with this sobering confession: "Those who cling to worthless idols turn away from God's love for them" (Jonah 2:8). And yet even there, in a place of isolation and helplessness, the Mercy King found him. God didn't abandon Jonah to the consequences of his idolatry. He heard his cry, lifted him from the depths, and gave him an opportunity for a fresh start. That is the mercy of God: patient, pursuing, and persistent, even when we run in the other direction.

If idolatry is the disease, worship is the cure. Our hearts were made to adore, and when we cast aside false gods, we must fill that space with the one who actually satisfies. Forsaking idols is not merely about denouncing misplaced loves; it is about awakening to the only love that has the strength and resolve to have and to hold us. It is shifting our gaze from fleeting distractions to the infinite beauty of Christ, the one who is worthy of every breath, every thought, and every longing of our hearts.

We were made for more than the empty chase. When we set our gaze on Jesus, we do not trade joy for duty; we trade chains for freedom, worry for peace, and hunger for satisfaction. Like the psalmist who declares, "Whom have I in heaven but you? And there is nothing on earth that I desire besides you" (Ps. 73:25 ESV), we discover that in Christ, we already have what our hearts have been searching for all along.

This is why he is the Mercy King. He is not just the antidote to our idolatry; he is the destination our hearts have always longed for. His mercy makes his rule desirable, and his authority makes his mercy powerful. The more we behold him, the more our idols lose their appeal. He rules not only because he is worthy but because he alone can save.

Therefore, for the love of God and for the sake of your soul, "Dear children, keep yourselves from idols" (1 John 5:21).

Summary

We are, by design, worshipers—always giving our hearts to someone or something. When God is not at the center, idols inevitably fill the void. These false gods—whether comfort, control, success, or approval—promise peace but lead to restlessness. Idolatry is more than misplaced affection, it is a deep fracture in our relationship with God, others, and ourselves. It begins subtly, grows quietly, and enslaves deeply. But Jesus, the Mercy King, does not leave us in our self-made prisons. He enters our stories not to scold us but to save us. With nail-scarred hands, he disarms our idols, heals our fractured hearts, and invites us into freedom. To turn from idols is not merely to reject deception but to respond to mercy—to rest in the one who is both strong enough to rescue and kind enough to restore.

Three Questions

1. Where do your thoughts, fears, or hopes most often drift when you're anxious or uncertain? What might that reveal about what your heart is trusting in?
2. How does the picture of Jesus as the Mercy King—both strong enough to defeat your idols and gentle enough to restore you—reshape your view of repentance?
3. What subtle shifts in your life (priorities, habits, or thought patterns) might be signs that your heart is quietly drifting toward something other than God? How might you respond today?

One Action Step

This week choose one recurring and intrusive thought, habit, or behavior that may be shaped by an idol (such as control, comfort, or approval). Each time it surfaces, pause and pray, "Lord, I surrender this to you. Reorder my loves. Help me trust that you alone are enough." Then replace that moment with a concrete truth from Scripture—such as Philippians 4:8 or Psalm 73:25—to realign your heart with the Mercy King, who reigns to redeem.

FOUR

When Comparison Steals Your Joy

The Mercy King Who Satisfies Your Heart

Envy is the ulcer of the soul.

—Socrates

Social media saturates life as we know it. We scroll through curated glimpses of each other's worlds—vacations, promotions, family moments, achievements—captured in highlight reels that seldom reflect the messier realities behind the scenes. But this exposure comes at a cost.

According to one study, approximately one in three individuals reported a decline in well-being after using social media, largely driven by envy, which in turn contributed to depressive symptoms.[1] Adjacent studies have also identified a connection between frequent social media usage and elevated anxiety, along with a decline in perceived emotional security. Another troubling effect has emerged as well: Many people now feel compelled to fabricate or exaggerate aspects of their lives online to keep up with the perceived successes of others.[2]

Other people's photos, in particular, can become powerful triggers for feelings of inadequacy, reminding us of what we lack. A friend's engagement or baby pictures may intensify feelings of loneliness or grief in those struggling with singleness or infertility. Holiday family gatherings, shared with joy, may deepen the grief of those experiencing estrangement or loss. Career milestone announcements can stir up feelings of failure and shame, highlighting someone else's sense of vocational stagnation. These insecurities can grow so intense that some people take social media breaks to shield themselves from the pangs of comparison and preserve their mental health.

But the ache goes deeper than screens and scrolling. The truth is, our envy doesn't begin with what we see, it begins with what we crave. Long before any of us were exposed to other people's highlight reels and filtered stories, the human heart was already restless, already longing, already aching for something more. The discontent we feel isn't new. It's as old as time. It's the quiet whisper that tells us that we don't have enough, that we are not enough, and that someone else has the life we were meant to live.

Envy is sneaky. It's an invisible thread that weaves its way through so many of our thoughts and feelings—resentment, insecurity, comparison, sadness. And yet it's not something we can simply will away. Left unchecked it distorts our desires, erodes our joy, and tempts us to believe that God is holding out on us.

And this is where Jesus, our gentle and merciful King, steps in. Not with condemnation but with compassion. He doesn't wait for us to clean up our envy or pretend it isn't there. He meets us in it. Right there, in the very place where our hearts feel most vulnerable and unsettled, he offers a better way: a life not ruled by comparison but anchored in his love. A kingdom built not on measuring up but on resting in the sufficiency of grace.

Jesus does not shame us for our discontent. He welcomes us in it. He invites us to bring our aching, envious hearts to him, and in return he offers wholeness where we once felt fractured.

In this chapter we'll explore four key aspects of envy and how, in each one, Jesus' presence and promises offer healing and hope.

First we will examine the lie that envy believes—the way it distorts reality, making us feel as if someone else's joy somehow diminishes our own. As we explored in the previous chapter on idolatry, idolatry is not just about worshiping false gods, it is about misplaced affections. At its core, envy is a form of idolatry. It is the heart bowing to another's real or perceived abundance instead of resting in the Lord's sufficiency. It is a false gospel, one that tells us our worth is found in having what others have rather than in being chosen by Christ.

Next we will identify the fuel that envy feeds on: the thought patterns and habits that deepen and sustain it.

Third we will explore the chaos that envy creates, revealing the harm it brings both personally and relationally.

Finally we will seek the way out—the pathway to peace, contentment, and a heart rooted in the freedom God desires for us.

The Lie That Envy Believes

At the heart of envy lives a quiet, persistent lie: If we had everything we wanted, then we would finally be happy. This is what makes envy so destructive. It's not just about wanting more, it's about believing that something in us is lacking. That if we could just close the gap—achieve more, acquire more, become more—then maybe the ache would go away.

Envy doesn't simply whisper, "I want what they have." It goes farther, suggesting, "I am less because I don't have it." It convinces us that we're overlooked, deficient, even defective. And all the while, Christ stands near—closer than we realize—with a mercy that whispers:

You are already chosen.

You are already beloved.

You already belong.

This is the heart of the Mercy King. He does not lead us into comparison, competition, or self-measurement. He leads us into rest. In his kingdom, value is not earned, hustled for, or lost to someone else's success. It is secure and settled, so we can be too. Our worth is determined not by how we stack up but by the price Jesus paid to make us his: his very own life.

Envy insists that joy and contentment are always out of reach, just one more achievement, one more possession, one more relationship away. But the gospel tells a different story. In Christ nothing essential is missing. In him we already have what we need most: love that doesn't waver, belonging that doesn't expire, and a future that doesn't depend on our performance.

The Mercy King doesn't wait for us to fix the ache of envy on our own. He enters into it. And there he reminds us—gently, patiently, again and again—that we are seen, we are secure, and we are already enough in him. Any "stinking thinking"[3] that says otherwise is what James, the half brother of Jesus and pastor of the early Jerusalem church, warns against.

In James 3:14–15, James describes the corrosive effects of "bitter envy and selfish ambition," which had overtaken many in the church, making them "earthly, unspiritual, and demonic." This cycle, however, is hardly unique to the first century. As nineteenth-century philosopher James Robert Boyd observed, envy arises when we feel uneasy at someone else's happiness or success, which often leads to resentment. Boyd's definition pinpoints how envy, at its core, opposes love. While love seeks the good of others, envy resents it. He adds that the cure for envy is contentment, learning to be satisfied with what we have, "whether we have much or little."[4]

Contentment, then, isn't dependent on circumstances but depends on the posture of our hearts.

Pastor and author Paul David Tripp offers a similar perspective, suggesting that envy stems less from external circumstances than from our "interpretation of the facts." Tripp argues that no one is more influential in our lives than we are, because no one speaks to us more than we do.[5]

Maybe you've felt it before, that pang of resentment when a friend gets the promotion you hoped for, the engagement you longed for, or the recognition you worked tirelessly to achieve. Maybe it's scrolling through social media late at night, feeling a quiet bitterness rise as others seem to move ahead while you stay stuck. Or perhaps you've tried to be happy for someone, only to feel that unwelcome sting of "why not me?" creeping in. Envy doesn't just steal joy. It isolates, leaving us ashamed of emotions we wish we didn't have.

This struggle isn't new, nor is it unique to us. Scripture speaks directly to these very moments when envy creeps in, urging us to feel unseen, unloved, and overlooked. James warns of the corrosive power of "bitter envy and selfish ambition" (James 3:14), a problem that plagued even the early church.

Constant comparison disrupts our ability to appreciate the uniqueness of our own lives, trapping us in a cycle of negativity and victimhood. This distortion of truth is central to envy's destructive power. Scripture repeatedly illustrates that contentment is achievable regardless of circumstances. Writing from prison, the apostle Paul in Philippians 4:12 declares that he has "learned the secret of being content in any and every situation," whether in abundance or in need. Remarkably, Paul notes the need to learn contentment even in times of plenty, not just in hardship. He understands that satisfaction doesn't automatically come with success or wealth; in fact, often the more we have, the more we crave.

Studies confirm this troubling dynamic. The *World Happiness Report 2025* ranked the United States—one of the wealthiest nations globally—twenty-fourth in happiness, behind places like Cost Rica and Mexico, where material resources were significantly scarcer. These findings suggest that happiness is linked not chiefly to wealth or success but to other things like social support, caring behaviors, generosity and strong community life, belief in the kindness of others, and one's inner state of mind and heart.[6]

The Fuel That Envy Feeds On

In Western culture, where the drive to achieve and win is relentless, many of us find ourselves constantly climbing, yet still feeling as though we've come up short. This cycle intensifies when we seek not just success but success in comparison with others. Envy doesn't simply desire what's good, it craves "more than" and "better than."

C. S. Lewis, in *Mere Christianity*, describes pride—the root of envy—as "essentially competitive." He writes, "Pride gets no pleasure out of having something, only out of having more of it than the next person. It's the pleasure of being above the rest."[7] Envy, fueled by this competitive pride, distorts our ability to love others well. Instead of celebrating others' successes, we resent them; rather than grieving in solidarity with those who suffer, we find secret pleasure in their misfortunes.

Envy rarely travels alone. It brings with it close companions: boasting and selfish ambition. As James explains, wherever envy is present, these behaviors follow, driven by a desire to outshine others. He doesn't soften his words; he calls this kind of envy "demonic," reminding us that it was envy that first corrupted God's good creation (James 3:15).

Scripture gives us two tragic examples of envy's origins. The first is the fallen angel Lucifer, who, despite being one of the most beautiful angels, could not accept his position as number two and craved equality with God. Puritan theologian Jonathan Edwards observes that envy made heaven itself unbearable for Lucifer, who sought his own glory and thus introduced evil into the universe. According to Edwards, "Satan fell by his envying the happiness of God's creatures, and by his pride in aspiring after it. Envy is that wherein his apostasy began. Envy made him uneasy in heaven. He could not bear to see the happiness of the saints and angels there, and therefore he became an enemy to it and sought their ruin."[8]

Similarly, envy played a central role in the fall of Adam and Eve. In the garden of Eden, history's first couple lived in perfect harmony with God and each other, surrounded by every good thing they needed. But when Satan tempted them, he appealed to their envy, suggesting that God was withholding something valuable by forbidding them to eat from the tree of knowledge. Satan's lie led them to believe they could be like God, no longer content with being his beloved, well-supported, generously provided-for creatures. They lost sight of the abundant blessings surrounding them, fixating instead on the one thing they were told they couldn't have.

In that moment even paradise wasn't enough.

In contrast Jesus, the true and better Adam, did not grasp for power and glory but humbled himself. Where envy led Adam and Eve to reach for a throne that was not theirs to take, Jesus gave up his rightful throne to meet us in our need. As the Mercy King, he confronts the curse envy unleashed, not by condemning us but by making himself nothing (Phil. 2:5–11).

Envy has always stolen joy, distorted identity, and driven people from God. But its destruction doesn't stop at our own hearts; it seeps into our relationships, sowing seeds of bitterness and division. The way out of envy's grasp is to recognize it as the lie it is, to stop believing that more and better will make us whole, and to anchor our contentment in the God who supplies all our needs according to his glorious riches in Christ (Phil. 4:19).

Envy does not just invite us to be miserable, it entices us to scoff at the King's abundance. When we envy we tell God that his gifts to us are not enough—that we deserve more, that he has mismanaged our portion. But if Christ is King, then we can trust that his distribution is always right. Our true satisfaction is not in having what others have. It is in belonging to the one who holds all things in his hands.

Scripture passages such as Psalm 73 can help awaken our souls to envy's destructiveness and the Mercy King's enough-ness:

> For I envied the arrogant
> when I saw the prosperity of the wicked. (v. 3)
>
> This is what the wicked are like—
> always free of care, they go on amassing wealth.
> (v. 12)
>
> Till I entered the sanctuary of God;
> then I understood their final destiny. (v. 17)
>
> You guide me with your counsel,
> and afterward you will take me into glory. (v. 24)
>
> My flesh and my heart may fail,
> but God is the strength of my heart
> and my portion forever. (v. 26)

> As for me, it is good to be near God.
> I have made the Sovereign Lord my refuge;
> I will tell of all your deeds. (v. 28)

The Chaos That Envy Creates

In a world ruled by envy, chaos is never far behind. But in the kingdom of the Mercy King, serenity takes root. Jesus doesn't pit us against one another, he welcomes us into a family. He doesn't ask us to prove our worth, he offers rest for our souls.

By its very nature envy fosters rage and disrupts peace. It's hard to imagine anyone saying envy has drawn them closer to God, deepened their joy, or strengthened their relationships. Whether it lingers quietly in our hearts or comes at us from others, it always leaves a wake of unrest. The deeper it goes, the more damage it does.

If envy is the thief of joy, Christ is joy's gracious restorer. But his answer isn't momentary relief or surface-level strategies. It's deeper, more transformative. He calls us to trust that in him, we already have enough. This is not just a shift in mindset, it's a rescue of the heart. Jesus doesn't stand at a distance, offering advice. He steps into our ache, carries the weight of our envy, and fills the emptiness with the riches of his love.

The way out from envy's grip isn't willpower. It's a reordering of our loves—from scarcity to sufficiency, from grasping to gratitude, from envying what others have to resting in what Christ gives. Only the Mercy King can lead us into this kind of transformation.

James writes, "For where you have envy and selfish ambition, there you find disorder and every evil practice" (James 3:16). And how true this is. Envy not only disturbs the soul, it poisons community. It corrodes relationships and sows discord. Scripture ties envy to practices like gossip, which at its core is a form of verbal exploitation. Gossip objectifies others, feeding on their flaws or misfortunes without any intent to love or restore. It may feel harmless—even gratifying and justified—but it's deeply destructive. Backbiting, cliques, manipulation—all forms of "vile practice"—create cultures of performance, where people feel pressure to curate façades rather than live with authenticity. These are not the fruit of the Spirit. They are symptoms of envy's presence.

Consider the story of a well-known actress and singer, admired and envied by many. Behind the applause and acclaim, she silently battled body image issues and the crushing pressure to meet impossible standards. She later shared how her inner critic was fueled by constant comparison—by the belief that no matter how rich, famous, and successful she became, it was never enough.

At the height of her fame, she prioritized weight loss over health, confessing that she practically lived at the gym to achieve a particular look. Yet even with all the striving and sacrifice, peace and self-acceptance remained out of reach.[9] Her story is painfully familiar in a culture fixated on perfection, where the pursuit of better often becomes a slow erosion of the soul. Comparison doesn't just distort how we see others, it distorts how we see ourselves.

Now contrast this with my friend David, who also cares deeply about his health, but for entirely different reasons. David's goal isn't image but stewardship. He wants to be present and strong for his family: to walk his daughter down the aisle, to lift his grandchildren, to serve God and his church as long as he's able. His motivation is love, not competition. While the actress felt crushed by comparison, David finds purpose in responsibility. One story is fueled by pressure, the other by calling. One isolates, the other connects. This is what envy does: It isolates and exhausts, squandering energy and joy.

Envy also clouds the mind. James describes it as "unspiritual"—from the Greek word *psychikos*, meaning devoid of sound judgment and spiritual clarity (James 3:15). Envy can drive us to obsessive fixation, making us lose sight of what matters most. Joseph Epstein once wrote, "Envy is absolutely no fun at all. It drains all joy from you from its very first moment."[10] The constant need to compare and compete is emotionally exhausting. Arthur Brooks, writing in *The New York Times*, adds that envy "pushes down life satisfaction and depresses well-being."[11] It's linked to anxiety, depression, even physical illness because of the emotional hostility it cultivates.

We see this vividly in the life of King Saul. Saul had slain his thousands—a remarkable accomplishment. But then David entered the picture, defeating Goliath with nothing but a sling and a stone. When the people sang, "Saul has slain his thousands, and David his tens of thousands" (1 Sam. 18:7), what should have been a shared moment of national pride turned bitter. From that day on Saul kept a jealous eye on David. And his envy began to unravel him.

Saul's obsession didn't just disturb him, it consumed him. He lost sight of his own calling, his own anointing, and instead fixated on someone else's. What made his downfall so tragic was that his envy revealed a deeper rebellion—not just against David but against God's wisdom and sovereignty. Envy distorted his faith, leading him to resist what God had ordained.

In time Saul's jealousy drove him to madness. He made multiple attempts on David's life. He became so preoccupied with David's success that he forfeited his own peace, his relationship with God, and ultimately his reign. Envy transformed a chosen king into a restless, bitter man. His story is a sobering reminder that comparison never leads to joy. It only deepens our grief.

Envy undermines peace. It distorts perception, damages relationships, and drains the soul. Instead of adding value, it subtracts, leaving us weary, dissatisfied, and hollow.

But in the kingdom of Christ, there is another way. A way where peace replaces discontentment, and where joy is found not in surpassing others but in being secure in the love of the one who holds all things together. In him we have enough. Under his kingship our grasping for more can cease because our value is no longer in question.

The Escape Door from Envy

In his letter James offers a powerful remedy for envy: "wisdom from above" (James 3:17 ESV). His message echoes the timeless insights found in Proverbs, urging believers toward lives marked by peace, humility, and integrity. For James, who was ultimately martyred for Christ, the antidote to envy is not a change in circumstances but a shift in perspective.

Envy thrives in the soil of dissatisfaction, while contentment rooted in wisdom from above grows and flourishes in the soil of gratitude. James describes the qualities of this heavenly wisdom as "pure . . . peaceable, gentle, open to reason, full of mercy and good fruits, impartial and sincere" (ESV). This wisdom cultivates a life where we can look at our circumstances—whether joyful or sorrowful—and find contentment, echoing the timeless hymn:

> When peace like a river attendeth my way;
> when sorrows like sea billows roll;
> whatever my lot, thou hast taught me to say
> it is well, it is well with my soul.[12]

Wisdom from above invites us to see both the triumphs and trials of life through God's eyes. Wisdom, then, is more than knowledge; it is the surrender of our interpretations and insecurities to the truth that God speaks over us and his creation.

Paul David Tripp observes that envy "ignores eternity." At its root, envy is not just about wanting what others have, it's about doubting that God's plan for us is good. It is a form of unbelief, a refusal to trust that God has given us exactly what we need for today. Envy fixates on lack and blinds us to the larger story God is writing. It ignores the happy ending and gets stuck in a middle chapter.

If we could fully grasp the glory awaiting us, envy would lose its grip. Few express this idea more poignantly than C. S. Lewis in *The Weight of Glory*:

> It is a serious thing to live in a society of possible gods and goddesses, to remember that the dullest most uninteresting person you can talk to may one day be a creature which, if you saw it now, you would be strongly tempted to worship. . . . It is in the light of these overwhelming possibilities, it is with the awe and the circumspection proper to them, that we should conduct all of our dealings with one another, all friendships, all loves, all play, all politics. There are no ordinary people. You have never talked to a mere mortal. Nations, cultures, arts, civilizations—these are mortal, and their life is to ours as the life of a gnat. But it is immortals whom we joke with, work with, marry, snub, and exploit—immortal horrors or everlasting splendors.[13]

The wisdom from above calls us to rest in the future God has secured for us, a future made certain by Christ's life, death, burial, and resurrection. Christ is the final answer to both our abundance and our lack. He will fulfill and surpass the best things in our lives and ultimately absorb the worst into an eternity where we will have all we truly desire.

Then and there, envy will no longer be possible.

Yet even now envy can cloud our vision of Christ's all sufficiency, twisting life into a story of scarcity rather than one of abundant grace. But Jesus, the Mercy King, reigns not by grasping but by giving. His kingdom is built not through accumulation but through his surrender. Unlike envy, which clings tightly and craves more, his mercy opens his hands—to release, to restore, and to redeem. He willingly laid down his glory so that we might receive what we could never earn. While envy resents the blessings others receive, Jesus rejoices in giving what none of us deserve.

In *God Is in the Manger*, Dietrich Bonhoeffer, writing from prison, reflects, "We are going to have an exceptionally good Christmas. Our response to every outward circumstance will show whether we can be content with what is truly essential." Even behind bars Bonhoeffer found his joy in Christ's sufficiency alone. Stripped of every earthly comfort, his suffering brought clarity about what truly matters. He prophetically declared, "The emptier our hands, the better we understand."

For Bonhoeffer, Christ's surrender and fullness eclipsed every earthly lack, revealing that contentment lies in the presence and provision of God.[14]

The wisdom from above, as James describes it, is not just a concept, it's embodied in the very life of Jesus. Like Lucifer, Jesus descended from heaven, but for entirely different reasons. Lucifer fell because he couldn't tolerate being second. Jesus, the firstborn over all creation and king of all kings, willingly stepped down from his throne not out of envy but out of love.

While Lucifer grasped for more, Jesus let go. He emptied himself, taking on the form of a servant, becoming poor, rejected, and humiliated not because he had to but because he wanted to make us whole. He chose the low place, the unenviable position, so we could be lifted into the arms of God and be called beloved.

This is the heart of the Mercy King. He made himself less so we could receive more. Not more status or more applause but more of him. More fullness, more wholeness, more gratitude.

So how do we break free of envy's grip? It starts by turning the volume up on one voice and down on another. In moments of disappointment and lack, we face a choice: Will we let the voice of envy fuel resentment and self-pity, or will we open ourselves to God's voice, affirming our worth in him? We can allow envy's whispers to suggest we are being shortchanged, or we can rest in the one who left paradise to secure our place in paradise. We can let the world's measures of success and worth define us, or we can trust that in Christ we are living the life he intends for us, for his glory and our ultimate good.

James tells us that true wisdom is pure, peaceable, gentle, full of mercy (James 3:17). This wisdom is not merely something to admire, it's an invitation to live differently. It calls us out of the anxious striving of comparison and into the quiet confidence of being known and loved by God.

So let's pause and ask, "What is envy costing me? Has it dimmed my joy? Eroded a friendship? Caused me to doubt that God sees me, knows me, or delights in me?" The fruits of envy are subtle, but deep seated: restlessness, resentment, and the nagging sense that someone else is living the life we were meant to have.

Wisdom offers a better way. While envy pulls us toward comparison, scarcity, and fatigue, wisdom leads us to peace, contentment, and trust. Envy whispers, "You're falling behind." Wisdom assures us, "You are right where you are meant to be." One path leaves us striving and empty, the other resting and full.

This is the way of Jesus, the Mercy King. He doesn't simply offer us freedom, he embodies it. He rules not through pressure or performance but through abundance and grace. In his kingdom our worth is not achieved, it is received. The grasping and measuring stops. The comparing and competing fades. And joy is no longer rooted in getting more but in receiving him.

So we ask again, "Will I keep chasing what can never satisfy, or will I receive what has already been given in full? Will I continue clinging to somebody else's lot, or will I lay down what was never mine to carry?"

His arms are open, his love is enough, and his invitation is clear:

Renounce comparing and competing.

Step into contentment.

Trust the King.

Summary

This chapter examines the all-consuming nature of envy—how it distorts our reality, fuels comparison, and robs us of joy. While social media amplifies these struggles, envy is not just a modern issue. It is a deep-seated condition of the human heart, one that has been at work since the beginning of time. We have seen envy turn blessings into burdens, disrupt relationships, and even lead to rebellion against God's will. Yet the answer to envy is found not in striving for more but in surrendering to the one who is already enough. Jesus, the Mercy King, does not merely offer relief from envy, he reigns over it. He calls us to step out of the cycle of comparison and into the freedom of his sufficiency. The question is, Will we keep chasing what can never satisfy, or will we trust the King who has already satisfied?

Three Questions

1. How does envy distort our perception of God, ourselves, and others?
2. In what ways has Jesus modeled the opposite of envy, and how does his example invite us into contentment?
3. What daily habits can help us cultivate gratitude and resist the pull of comparison?

One Action Step

Each day this week, take a moment to identify and write down three things you are grateful for, based not on achievements, possessions, or comparisons but on the goodness of God in your life. Let this practice train your heart to focus on what is already yours in Christ, rather than on what you feel you lack.

MOVEMENT TWO

The Hurts We Endure

FIVE

When Suffering Shakes Your Faith

The Mercy King Who Heals What We Cannot

> The way that Jesus treated women tore up the belief that women are innately inferior to men: a belief that was pervasive in the ancient world.
>
> —Rebecca McLaughlin, *Jesus Through the Eyes of Women*

What kind of leader draws near to those who are in pain, speaks tenderly to those who are outcast, and willingly pauses for someone society has rendered invisible? Only one: Jesus, the Mercy King. His way is marked not by sentimental softness but by royal authority that uses power to restore dignity, reverse despair, and reign through compassion.

Across all four gospels, Jesus, the Mercy King, is portrayed as a miraculous healer, a physician like no other. As the opening quote of this book reminds us, "The hands of the king are the hands of a healer, and so shall the rightful king be known."[1]

Throughout his ministry, people were drawn to Jesus not only because he was willing to heal but because he was able to. No sickness or sorrow was beyond his reach. When he said, "Be healed," healing came, fully and without delay. Mark's gospel in particular offers repeated glimpses of this restorative power: Jesus raises a paralyzed man, heals a withered hand, and gives sight to a man who had been born blind. He silences wind and waves as though they were an unruly child, and he casts out demons, bringing lasting peace to tortured minds and hearts.

In the passage we'll explore in this chapter—Mark 5:21–43—we encounter two people, vastly different in circumstance, but united in desperation. Both come to Jesus longing for his mercy, his healing touch, and the kind of hope that only the true and rightful King can offer.

Jairus, a synagogue ruler, pleads for his dying daughter. As both a father and a respected religious leader, he likely tried every possible solution before coming to Jesus, making his plea all the more urgent and vulnerable. The second is a woman suffering from a chronic bleeding disorder, a condition she has endured for as long as Jairus's daughter has been alive. She approaches Jesus differently, quietly and anonymously, and her story becomes intertwined with his, revealing even more about the Mercy King's compassion and power.

Jesus' response to these two individuals challenges three common misconceptions about suffering: that he does too little, that he asks too much, and that he is out of touch. Through these two intertwined stories, he dismantles these doubts and reveals that his delays are not neglect, his demands are not cruelty, and his silence is not absence. We're asked to trust that his mercy reigns, even when we don't understand.

The Questions That Haunt Us

As much as these stories stir awe, they also stir something else: honest, lingering questions. If Jesus is this powerful, this compassionate, why do we still suffer? Why does he delay? Why doesn't he heal everyone who asks? Scripture doesn't offer easy answers. Instead it invites us into a deeper trust by showing us that while Jesus holds the power to heal, he often moves in ways and timing we wouldn't expect.

Take Jacob, for example. After wrestling with God, he walked away not with a triumphant victory but with a limp—a lasting reminder of his encounter with the Almighty—even as he stepped into his calling as the father of Israel's twelve tribes (Gen. 32:22–32). Or consider the apostle Paul. Tormented by what he called a "thorn in my flesh," he pleaded with God for relief. But God didn't remove the suffering. Instead he said, "My grace is sufficient for you, for my power is made perfect in weakness" (2 Cor. 12:7–10). That answer reshaped Paul's entire outlook. What once felt like a liability became a window through which he could see God's strength most clearly. He began to rejoice in hardship not because pain had vanished but because grace had taken root.

We see this same paradox in the life of Ludwig van Beethoven. One of history's most masterful composers, Beethoven began to lose his hearing in his late twenties, an unthinkable affliction for someone whose vocation depended entirely on sound. The silence was not just physical. It plunged him into a season of despair so deep he once wrote of feeling hopeless and isolated, even contemplating ending his life.

And yet in that very silence something astonishing occurred.

After Beethoven's hearing loss became most severe, Beethoven went on to compose some of his most transcendent music. His Ninth Symphony—home to the iconic "Ode to Joy"—was written when he was functionally deaf.

Joy through deafness? What kind of joy is that?

His story echoes pastoral conversations I've had over the years with women and men devastated by betrayal. I've sat with spouses crushed by unfaithfulness, their hearts splintered by grief. And yet through tears and trembling faith, some have spoken of a peace they didn't manufacture, a Spirit-given grace that surprised them. Even more astounding, many have expressed a willingness—born not of willpower but of the mercy of Jesus—to forgive. Not because the pain was small but because mercy had reached into the darkest places and done what only mercy can do.

This is the way of the Mercy King. He doesn't only repair what is broken, he enters the brokenness with us. Sometimes his deepest healing comes not by reversing the wound but by remaking us through it. He brings joy not by skipping over sorrow but by planting it in the soil of our pain and sorrow, where somehow, mysteriously, it grows.

The stories of Jairus and the bleeding woman invite us into this tension. And they invite us to confront three false beliefs, subtle misconceptions that often arise in seasons of suffering. But before we examine those, consider this question:

If forced to choose between the two, would you rather have Jesus change your circumstances, or your heart?

We know that for those who trust in him, Jesus will one day change both, bringing complete healing in the new heaven and new earth (Rev. 21:1–8). But if he were to say, "From now until the day you die, or until I return, I will change either your situation or your heart," which would you choose? What would your answer be?

Some of us might be tempted to choose relief over renewal, to change the situation and save the inner work for later. But Jesus offers more than we often think to ask for. As Paul reminds us in Ephesians 3:20, the Mercy King is able to do far more than we ask or imagine. And as C. S. Lewis once observed, our desires are often too small for a world governed by God. "We are far too easily pleased," he wrote.[2]

This is the tension in which we live: the space between wanting change and needing transformation. And it's in this space that misconceptions about God often take hold. We start to wonder, Is he listening? Does he care? Is he doing anything at all?

These questions are not new. They echo through the hearts of those who suffer, and three false beliefs emerge. The first false belief that often surfaces is that Jesus does too little.

False Belief 1: Jesus Does Too Little

Our first misconception is that Jesus does too little. In both the story of Jairus's daughter and the story of the woman with the bleeding condition, Jesus allows prolonged suffering, longer than either would have chosen. And yet those delays are not signs of neglect but part of his healing work. By allowing desperation to deepen, he brings healing not only to the body but also to the heart.

When it comes to healing, God often uses two kinds of means: the ordinary and the miraculous. We see both in this passage. For those of us in places like Nashville—sometimes called the "Silicon Valley of health care"—this resonates deeply. Many in our churches and communities labor each day to ease suffering. Thanks to modern medicine, a cardiologist can guide a tiny camera through a heart, place a stent, and send a patient home by dinner. These marvels are ordinary means, yet still gifts from God.

And still even the best medicine has limits. Each Sunday, pastors look into congregations filled with people who, like the woman in Mark 5, have tried everything. After twelve years of suffering, her health has worsened. She has spent all she has. She's exhausted and isolated. Her story mirrors the ache of many today.

Having served as a pastor for thirty years, I've witnessed the toll of unhealed suffering. Often people turn to Jesus only when every other option has failed. But here is the good news: Even when we come to him as a last resort, Jesus meets us not with disappointment but with compassion. He welcomes our desperate prayers even when our faith feels tattered and small.

For the bleeding woman, physical suffering is only part of her pain. Her condition has left her ceremonially unclean, cut off from touch, community, and dignity. While Jairus approaches Jesus publicly and with status, she comes in secret—ashamed, unnoticed, and uncertain of her worth. Her faith is real, but hesitant. She doesn't stand tall before Jesus. She reaches from behind, hoping not to be seen.

But Jesus refuses to let her remain hidden.

In a culture where women are often known only by their relationships—daughter of, wife of, mother of—this woman has been known only by her affliction. For twelve long years, she's had no advocate, no voice, no name that carries affection. But Jesus gives her one. With a single word—daughter—he restores what suffering has taken. He names her not by what she's endured but by what she's worth.

This is more than a healing. It's a royal decree.

Her identity isn't explained, earned, or negotiated. It is bestowed. This is how the Mercy King reigns: by restoring what has been stolen and naming those who feel forgotten. He does not merely heal bodies, he reclaims souls. He wields power not to dominate but to mend and make whole.

Jairus's need is no less urgent. His daughter is dying. A respected synagogue leader, he humbles himself before Jesus with a plea that sounds like both a father's anguish and a disciple's hope: "Come lay your hands on her, so she may be made well and live." Every second matters. He has rushed through the streets, Jesus by his side.

And now, as Jesus stops to tend to another, Jairus waits—helpless, watching the clock.

And then the news comes: "Your daughter is dead."

What must that moment have felt like? The urgency had been real. The hope had been fragile. And now it seemed too late.

But Jesus operates on a different timeline, one in which delays are not denials but designs for deeper healing. By the time they reach the house, mourners are already weeping. When Jesus says, "She's not dead; she's sleeping," they laugh. It sounds absurd. But Jesus sees what they cannot: Death is no match for his mercy.

Only a King with cosmic authority can speak to death as though it were sleep. Jesus doesn't panic, he commands. His calm isn't indifference, it's sovereignty wrapped in love. He reigns over time, over decay, and even over the grave.

This scene echoes the grief and disorientation many of us feel in our own seasons of suffering. When God delays, when prayers go unanswered, when hope dims, we wonder whether he cares at all. The silence can feel unbearable. In moments like these we may resonate not with the heroes of faith but with those like Job's wife. After losing ten children in a single day, she cries out in anguish, "Curse God and die." Her words are often judged harshly, but who could endure such loss without despair?

Her pain is real. Her lament, raw. And while her words may falter, they reflect a wound that the Mercy King understands.

A surprising and sobering example of feeling abandoned by God in the midst of deep faith can be found in the life of Mother Teresa. Known around the world for her tireless work among the poor in Calcutta, she privately carried a burden few knew about—a heavy and prolonged sense of spiritual emptiness. In letters to her spiritual advisors, published after her death, she describes what she calls a "dark night of the soul," marked by years of sensing God's absence.

"I feel that God does not want me, that God is not God, and that he does not really exist," she once wrote.

For Mother Teresa, the silence wasn't occasional, it was constant. She longed for Jesus' presence, yet often encountered only a sense of distance and void. It felt at times as though Christ had hidden his face. And yet in the absence of emotional reassurance, she continued to pray, serve, and persevere. Her life became a quiet, unwavering witness to a faith that often shines brightest not in clarity but in darkness.

Even in her struggle, she found a kind of fellowship with Christ—not through relief or resolution but through shared suffering. Her ache echoed Jesus' cry on the cross: "My God, my God, why have you forsaken me?" Identifying with that cry, she discovered a mysterious solidarity, a deeper connection with the one who bore abandonment for our sakes.

Her story reminds us that faith is not always accompanied by felt assurance. Sometimes it looks like showing up, loving others, and holding on, especially when God feels silent. Mother Teresa's perseverance bears witness to this: that Christ's redeeming love will ultimately transform all sorrow, even when it seems hidden in the moment.

This is the paradox of faith: It endures even when it cannot feel. And the question it leaves us with is this: When we face our own dark nights of the soul, will we press into God, or will we pull away?

To live in despair or to die in unbelief is a tragedy far deeper than suffering itself. When we place conditions on our faith, expecting God to meet our expectations before we extend trust, we risk disillusionment. We begin to relate to him not as children but as consumers.

It's like a child at the doctor's office. Imagine them squirming and crying as a parent gently restrains them so a nurse can administer a shot. In that moment, the child feels confused, maybe even betrayed. Why would someone who loves them allow this pain? But the parent knows this brief sting is a small price for something far greater: health, protection, long-term good.

In the same way, our suffering may feel like abandonment, but often it is love we don't yet understand. God is not indifferent. When it seems like God is holding us down or holding us back, in reality he is simply holding us—often unseen, always securely. What feels like absence will in time reveal itself as a deeper presence.

We may think he is doing too little.

But he is doing far more than we can comprehend.

False Belief 2: Jesus Asks Too Much

Our second misconception is the belief that Jesus asks too much of us. His expectations can feel impossibly high, especially when he asks us to do two things we are inclined to resist:

Wait.

And trust.

First he asks us to wait. For how long? The Lord's answer is both unsettling and unambiguous: "As long as I decide." The timeline is his alone to set, know, and control. And we won't know the waiting is over until he says so. As Tom Petty famously sang, "The waiting is the hardest part."[3] Waiting on God stretches our patience, tests our faith, and exposes the illusion that we are in control.

Jairus was accustomed to being heard and responded to quickly. He held status, influence, and authority, things that often serve as a "fast pass" through life. Surely if anyone commanded Jesus' immediate attention, it was him. His daughter was dying, for goodness' sake.

But Jesus doesn't operate on the logic of urgency.

He is the master of lengthy pauses.

In today's world, if a doctor prioritized a nonemergency over a critical case, it would be labeled malpractice and their license might be suspended or revoked. Jairus likely felt something similar as he watched Jesus pause for someone who, by all appearances, could wait, while his own daughter lay on the brink of death. The delay must have felt unbearable. Every second stretched the anguish and bewilderment.

Then comes the second thing Jesus asks of us: trust.

Early in my faith, I memorized Proverbs 3:5–6: "Trust in the Lord with all your heart and lean not on your own understanding." At age nineteen those words felt inspiring and straightforward. But over time, life has a way of revealing how hard trust really is. With each loss, disappointment, or unraveling plan, trust becomes less about certainty regarding desired outcomes and more about surrender to the wild, untamable mysteries of God.

A scene from the TV series *1883* captures this sobering shift. A mother turns to her daughter—young, hopeful, still seeing the world with wonder—and says, "I wish I could still see the world through your eyes." Then with gentle sorrow she adds, "But someday, you're going to see the world through mine."[4]

The hard and heavy stuff of life teaches us that this world is not as it should be. And it's into this brokenness that Jesus quietly invites our trust.

The prophet Isaiah reminds us why: "'My thoughts are not your thoughts, neither are your ways my ways,' declares the Lord" (Isa. 55:8–9). For Jairus this means relinquishing control, something deeply unfamiliar for a man accustomed to being in charge and getting results. As Tim Keller once wrote, "The hardest thing to give up is control,"[5] especially for those who are used to enjoying it. Most of the time it requires a crisis to finally loosen our grip.

It's as if Jesus is saying to Jairus (and to us), "You're living under an illusion, one that if not lovingly disrupted will lead to a far deeper crisis than the one you're facing now. The truth is, you've never truly been in control. Your resources, education, and influence may offer comfort, but they cannot shield you from life's uncertainties. Letting go of the illusion isn't failure, it's freedom. It's the threshold into something richer and more real. This is how I prepare you for the world that is coming, the world without end. If your heart never aches for that world, especially in the sorrows of this one, you may miss it altogether. And that, more than any earthly loss, would be the greatest tragedy. When you arrive in heaven, I don't want it to feel like a stranger's house. I want it to feel like home, like something your soul has already started to know. The pain you endure now, and the longing it awakens, are not wasted. They are the way I'm getting you ready."

To Jairus it may have felt like Jesus was wielding a sword. But in truth he was holding a scalpel, performing a surgery on his soul. The Mercy King always acts with purpose, on purpose. He delays not to rub salt in the wound but to heal it more deeply. His timing may seem insensitive to our urgency, but it is always shaped by love and the long view.

God knows what it means to lose a child. The cross bears witness to that. So when Jairus weeps, Jesus doesn't stand aloof, he draws near. And yet even in his nearness, he doesn't abandon his purpose or adjust his pace. Jairus wants rescue. Jesus offers that and much more with the promise of resurrection.

He's not simply healing a daughter's "sleeping" body. He's awakening a father's soul.

And so his invitation comes not as a demand: "Stay with me. Trust me."

Then the Lord of body and soul turns to the bleeding woman. Unlike Jairus, she expects to be ignored. She is no stranger to loss. For twelve years she has suffered—her body broken, her dignity eroded. She is an outcast, a name no one calls.

If Jairus represents the powerful and prioritized, she represents the powerless and overlooked.

Jairus is a man in a male-dominated world; she is a woman, unnoticed.

Jairus is wealthy; she is destitute.

Jairus is polished and respected; she is unclean and discarded.

Jairus stands with status; she crawls, covered with blood and dirt.

And yet in this upside-down kingdom, the Mercy King sees them both. He stops for both. He heals both. But he turns to her first.

Despite the stark contrast between them—or perhaps because of it—Jesus asks the powerful, respected man to wait while he gives his full attention to the desperate, isolated woman. In a world obsessed with status and pecking orders, his decision to prioritize her before him speaks volumes. She is not an interruption. She is an image-bearer of God, fully worthy of love, dignity, and care.

To onlookers this moment might seem alarming and inappropriate. But this is no ordinary kingdom. The Mercy King moves with sovereign freedom not to flatter the powerful but to lift up the weak. He reorders who gets seen and tended to first, and in doing so reveals his nature and heart.

Jesus' actions uncover a hidden grace:

For those used to winning, sometimes the greatest mercy is to wait.

For those used to waiting, the greatest mercy is to be seen, valued, and restored.

This woman's healing is about more than just her physical condition; it's about restoring her dignity, her sense of worth, and her place in the community. Jesus doesn't just heal her body, he heals her heart, affirming that her value isn't diminished by her suffering.

Jairus's story speaks tenderly to those who like him are familiar with success and accustomed to things going their way. For those who are used to leading, solving, and achieving, the deepest healing often begins not in strength but in crisis, in that place of unexpected vulnerability where self-sufficiency falls short and deeper need is revealed. Having pastored communities filled with high achievers for decades, I've seen how difficult this message can be to receive. I've also experienced that difficulty many times myself. And yet there are times when the most redemptive thing that can happen to us is not to prevail but to be led to the end of ourselves, because it's often there that mercy begins its most powerful work.

In the end, Jesus assures Jairus that he hasn't forgotten him or his precious daughter. Through waiting he will receive something far more than he asked for. Jesus' delay was not indifference; it was preparation for a miracle that would deepen Jairus's understanding of who Jesus is. Instead of merely resuscitating the girl, Jesus waits for her to die so he can resurrect her. And the woman who felt invisible in the crowd is about to experience her own miracle: being seen, known, and loved by the one who heals both body and soul.

False Belief 3: Jesus Is out of Touch

Mother Teresa's private struggle with doubt reflects an experience many of us share in moments of our own desperation: We believe that Jesus has the power to help us, yet when we cry out in our darkest hours, he seems silent. This silence can stir unsettling questions: With all his power, why doesn't God make things easier for us? Does he see our suffering? Does he even care?

This all gets put into perspective when we realize that while our pain is involuntary, Jesus chose a path of unimaginable hardship. With a heart burdened by grief, his body battered and bloodied on the merciless cross, the Mercy King opened a way for our lives to be transformed by his grace. Through his own suffering, he opened the door for us to find hope, healing, and redemption in ours.

This idea of Jesus' sharing in our suffering is powerfully illustrated in the story of the bleeding woman. The moment she touches the hem of his garment, her bleeding stops. Yet where her suffering ends, Jesus' suffering begins. Power leaves him and weakness sets in. "Who touched my clothes?" He asks because in that moment he realizes that power has gone out of him. This is not just a moment of miraculous healing, it is a foreshadowing of the cross. Every wound the Mercy King would bear, every rejection he would endure, every drop of blood he would shed—each would be an exchange, absorbing our sin and sickness while transferring to us his saving health.

Isaiah speaks to this exchange: "By his wounds we are healed" (Isa. 53:5–6). When Jesus' strength goes out from him, his suffering mysteriously becomes our relief. Every blessing and healing we experience costs him something. When the woman is healed, he lets go of some of his power temporarily—a preview of the ultimate price he will pay on the cross, where he will give up everything for our sakes.

Consider too how Jesus responds to mockery later in his ministry. In Nazareth, his hometown, he says, "No prophet is accepted in his hometown" (Luke 4:24), predicting that people will eventually say to him, "Physician, heal yourself." Ten chapters later, at his crucifixion, people sneer, "He saved others, but he can't save himself" (Mark 15:31). When they demand, "Physician, heal yourself," Jesus' answer is a silent refusal. He chooses not to save himself so that he can save us. He willingly subjects himself to poverty, rejection, humiliation, and pain—even unto death—to pass on to us his life and peace.

In healing, Jesus also takes on our defilement. As mentioned earlier, under Old Testament law, anyone who touched a bleeding person or a corpse became ceremonially unclean. Normally, purity was fragile: when something clean touched something unclean, it was the clean that became contaminated. But with Jesus the opposite happens. When he touches the bleeding woman, she becomes clean, and he willingly bears her impurity. It's a merciful exchange—one that also foreshadows the cross, where he took upon himself all our corruption as though it were his own.

Jesus doesn't merely meet us in our brokenness, he enters it, carries it, and lifts us out of it. And he gives more than just the hem of his garment. He clothes us in the full robe of his righteousness (Isa. 61:10), covering us not with shame and condemnation but with honor and grace.

When Jesus raises Jairus's daughter, he does more than prolong her life. He points to something far greater. Doctors and healers can delay death, but they cannot prevent it. The resuscitated daughter of the synagogue ruler, like the woman who suffered for twelve years, eventually passed away. Their resuscitations were temporary signs of a future promise: the resurrection. Jesus' command to Jairus's daughter, "Arise," is a glimpse of his own resurrection on the first Easter, when he will become the "firstfruits of those who have fallen asleep" (1 Cor. 15:20 ESV).

For those who trust in Christ, death is not an end but a new beginning. Christians are not buried, they are planted, like seeds holding the promise of new life. In light of this, our prayers for healing should reflect this larger hope: "Lord, not *if* it is your will but *according to* your will—whether in this life or in eternity—heal this person." God promises that in the final resurrection, all pain, tears, and death will be erased, and all of our fears will finally be gone.

Our role now is to respond to Jesus' call to Jairus: "Do not fear, only believe." For those who don't know Jesus, there is no lasting hope that anyone telling the truth can offer. But for those who place their trust in him, even as a last resort, that trust is sufficient. The

Mercy King is always ready to restore dignity and bring new life to those who seek him, no matter how beaten down they may feel.

A prayer once offered by a friend during a dark, desperate season in his life captures this hope. With bruises on his heart that he will carry for the rest of his life, he prayed, "Merciful Father, heal our hurts, but not without the healing of our hearts."

How could anyone pray such a thing unless, as Tolkien wrote, they truly believed that in the end "everything sad will come untrue"?[6] And yet that is the very promise: Everything sad *will* come untrue. Even if solutions don't come in this lifetime, his promises remain. For every believer in Christ, the long-term *worst*-case scenario is resurrection, complete healing of body and soul, and everlasting life.

Jesus doesn't merely respond to our needs. He sets out to transform our deepest wounds into hope, even as he leads us toward a future where perfect wholeness and joy will never end.

Waiting is hard. Pain rarely makes sense in the moment. But as Jairus learned, and as the bleeding woman experienced, Jesus is never absent; he is always working, always moving, even when his silence becomes deafening to us. The delays that feel unbearable to us may, in the hands of the Mercy King, be the very places where faith is deepened, where trust is formed, and where healing—seen or unseen—takes its deepest root.

So in the waiting, in the confusion, in the moments when Jesus seems too late, let's dare to believe his mercy is never absent and his love is never too slow.

And when the time is right, he will turn to you, call you daughter or son, and remind you once again: You were never forgotten.

Summary

Jairus, a respected leader, and an unnamed woman, cast to the margins, both come to Jesus in desperation. Though they are worlds apart in status, Jesus meets them with the same attentive mercy. But he also makes them wait. His timing stretches their faith, subverts expectations, and reveals that his delays are not dismissals but invitations to deeper trust. Jesus is not only a healer of bodies but the Mercy King, one who restores identity, upends social hierarchies, and brings resurrection where there was once only loss. His pace may feel slow, but it is never careless. Whether through waiting, weeping, or wonder, he is always working—refining our trust, reshaping our longings, and preparing us for the world without end.

Three Questions

1. Where do you feel tempted to believe that Jesus is doing too little? What emotions rise to the surface when his timing doesn't align with your desires?
2. Who do you relate to more right now—Jairus, used to being heard and helped, or the bleeding woman, accustomed to being unseen? How does Jesus' response to each reshape your view of his mercy?
3. What would it mean to trust not just in Jesus' power but in his pace? How might surrendering your timeline to him open you to a deeper kind of healing?

One Action Step

This week identify one area where you feel eager for change or healing. Instead of rushing to fix it, practice resting in the presence of the one who sees, knows, and cares. Each day offer this simple prayer as a way of letting go and leaning in:

> *Lord, here is the place where I am waiting. I long for resolution, but more than that, I long to trust you. Help me believe that your mercy is not missing just because I can't see the outcome yet. Make me whole—whether through healing or through hope—as I wait with you.*

SIX

When You Can't Forgive Yourself

The Mercy King Who Redeems Lost Causes

> I do not understand the mystery of grace—only that it meets us where we are and does not leave us where it found us.
>
> —Anne Lamott, *Traveling Mercies*

An election season has a way of bringing out the worst in all of us. The debates grow louder, the rhetoric sharper, and soon it feels like nearly everyone is caught up in the frenzy. But if we step back, we realize this is nothing new.

Political contests have always been intense. Consider, for example, the British election of 1868, a fiercely charged moment in history. At its center stood two towering figures: William Gladstone and Benjamin Disraeli. Each offered a distinct vision for the future, and each commanded national attention.

Amid the political fervor was Jennie Jerome, the future mother of Winston Churchill, renowned for her wit and influence. She announced that she would dine with both candidates and share her impressions publicly. The public eagerly awaited her verdict.

After dining with Gladstone, she remarked, "After sitting next to Gladstone, I thought he was the cleverest man in England." Few would have disagreed. But her dinner with Disraeli left a different impression. "After sitting next to Disraeli, I thought I was the cleverest woman in England," she said.

Her words captured something essential about Disraeli's leadership: his ability to help others feel seen, heard, and valued. That quality resonated deeply, and though he did not win in 1868, it helped carry him to victory in 1874.[1]

We are drawn to leaders who remind us that we matter. We long for wisdom, steadiness, and someone who understands our hopes and needs. Yet even history's finest leaders, for all their strengths, remain human, limited in time, wisdom, and power.

Jesus, the Mercy King, is different.

His authority is not granted by popularity or sustained by public approval. He does not seek votes or angle for our allegiance. He is not King because we elect him. He is King because he is. His reign cannot be challenged or overthrown. His mercy does not fluctuate with polls or approval ratings. He governs not from a distance but up close—attuned, present, and personal.

He doesn't rely on charisma, polished speeches, or partisan spin. When you encounter him, you're not just aware of his brilliance. You feel, somehow, like the most important person in the world.

This is the kind of King who enters the life of an unlikely, even despised, figure: Zacchaeus.

Zacchaeus was a tax collector, and not just any tax collector but a chief among them. His neighbors saw him as a traitor, a cheat, a man beyond redemption. Most had long since written him off. But

Jesus didn't. He looked up, called him by name, and invited himself in. Before Zacchaeus could offer allegiance, Jesus offered kindness. Before he could prove anything, Jesus extended mercy.

And this is the heart of the Mercy King.

In Zacchaeus's story, we see both the crown and the compassion of Jesus—the ruling hand of a King and the tender touch of a Shepherd. This is no mere encounter with a prophet or teacher. It is a brush with divine royalty.

In the pages ahead we'll walk through Zacchaeus's transformation and witness how one encounter with the Mercy King can give a bad man a new name. And once that new name is spoken, it does something remarkable: It rewrites his story—and ours as well—from the inside out.

Let's begin by taking a closer look at Zacchaeus's deeply flawed, and surprisingly redeemable, life.

A Bad Man in a Tree

Zacchaeus wasn't your average tax collector. He was the chief. A man of authority with the full backing of Rome, he had been entrusted with collecting revenue for the empire but used the role not only to meet Rome's demands but to enrich himself along the way.

As my father used to say, "There are two kinds of people in this world: givers and takers." Zacchaeus, beyond any shadow of doubt, was a taker. And not discreetly. He didn't skim quietly or hide behind polite ambition; he took openly and unapologetically, amassing wealth at the expense of everyone around him.

The system made it easy. Tax collectors were expected to gather what was owed, but they were also free to collect more and pocket the surplus. There were no regulations, no oversight, just the boundaries of one's own conscience. And Zacchaeus's conscience, from all appearances, had long since been numbed, if not silenced. His income was limited only by how much public hatred he could stomach and how many glares he could endure.

But did it satisfy him?

He had spent years hardening his heart, convincing himself that wealth was enough—that power could replace belonging and that fear was just another form of respect. Yet on nights when the streets were quiet, when there were no crowds to sneer at him and no coins left to count, did he ever feel the ache of what he'd lost? Did he ever long for someone to see him not as a tax collector or a villain but simply as a man? Someone more than the worst thing he had done?

Whatever he felt, he kept going. With every ill-gotten coin, his fortune grew, one bitter glance at a time. As chief tax collector he would have surrounded himself with deputies cut from the same cloth: men who took freely, openly, and without apology.

His wealth afforded him luxuries few in Jericho could dream of: fine clothes, lavish meals, a home perched high above the city. But for all his success, no one looked up to him. Not with admiration. Not even physically, for Zacchaeus was also short in stature. On the day he climbed that tree to catch a glimpse of Jesus, he remained unseen and ignored by a crowd that could barely stand the sight of him.

But perhaps that was nothing new.

Maybe Zacchaeus had spent years telling himself that isolation didn't matter—that wealth was a fair trade for love, and public disdain was just the cost of doing business. But in the quiet of his extravagant home, surrounded by every proof of success, did he ever wonder whether something was missing? Did he ever feel that no amount of silver could quiet the ache inside?

Maybe he climbed that tree not just to see Jesus but to be seen by him. To know, for the first time in a long time, that he was not beyond reach.

Then something unexpected happened.

The crowd was moving, surging forward as Jesus passed beneath the tree. Zacchaeus's breath caught. Maybe it was foolish to think Jesus would notice him. Maybe, like everyone else, he would look right past him—or worse, call him out with public shame.

But Jesus stopped.

He noticed Zacchaeus first. He looked up, called him by name, and spoke, not with judgment but with welcome. Jesus took the initiative not only as a compassionate friend but as the Mercy King, reclaiming a hostage from captivity. Unlike Jairus in the previous chapter, Zacchaeus held a high position but carried no esteem. Yet here he was, given the gift of a friend, an advocate, and the chance to begin again.

Jesus didn't just see him. He called him—personally, publicly, and with the full weight of divine authority. Yet there was no rebuke in his voice, no conditions to meet. Just an invitation, spoken with kindness.

What kind of King calls out the disgraced by name and dines with them like friends?

Only a Mercy King.

And just like that, a man who had spent his life taking was suddenly ready to give.

Scandalous Grace and Social Backlash

But not everyone was celebrating. Jesus had crossed a line. He was associating with the very kind of person respectable people avoided. In Jericho, Zacchaeus was considered scum—irreversibly compromised and morally bankrupt. The accepted response was to keep him at a distance. But Jesus did the opposite. He moved toward him.

In a culture that prized separation between the clean and the unclean, the respectable and the rejected, Jesus violated social norms to extend grace. His actions said what words could not:

In God's kingdom there is no division between the good and the bad.

There is only the humble and the proud.

For the proud, that truth was hard to swallow. But for the humble, it was life giving.

Luke, the gospel writer, highlights this pattern again and again. Tax collectors, universally loathed, are repeatedly brought to the forefront in a positive light. In chapter 3 they come forward to be baptized. In chapter 5 Jesus calls Matthew, a tax collector, to be his disciple, asking no questions about his past. In chapter 7 they are portrayed as receptive to Jesus' message. In chapter 15 Jesus tells the parable of the prodigal son while surrounded by tax collectors and sinners. And now, in chapter 19, the ultimate scandal: Salvation arrives at the house of the chief tax collector himself.

This new reality—where even someone like Zacchaeus is embraced—is both beautiful and offensive. It rattled those who clung to religious pride, and it still does. Jesus shattered the lines people had drawn between "us" and "them," between those who belonged and those who didn't.

His radical inclusion continues to unsettle. It challenges our assumptions and comforts our shame. It breaks down the very walls we're so quick to build.

For Zacchaeus, that likely grand home—once a symbol of taking, of power, of exclusion—was about to become the setting of a miracle. His heart, long hardened by wealth and self-interest, was being reshaped by scandalous grace. In just a few hours he would realize what the gospel has always offered: that grace is not only for those who play by the rules.

It's also for people like him—for the outlaws, the overlooked, the unexpected.

Zacchaeus wasn't alone in his taking spirit. His story is part of a much larger tapestry, a long line of questionable characters whom God not only noticed but pursued and redeemed. People with histories marked by failure and sometimes by grievous wrongdoing.

Take King David, for instance. His legacy as Israel's greatest king and beloved psalmist is secure. His words have comforted generations. But his story is far more complicated. Behind the psalms is a man who also orchestrated betrayal, abuse, and death. David's story with Bathsheba isn't just a cautionary tale about a moral lapse. It's a story of power misused. It began with David seeing Bathsheba, the wife of his loyal soldier Uriah, bathing on a rooftop. He sent for her, took her, and left her without a choice. And the fallout? When Bathsheba became pregnant, David sought to cover his tracks. He arranged for Uriah's death, dragging Bathsheba into a web of deceit designed to preserve his reputation.

This wasn't the act of a noble man. It was the act of a man trapped in a web of his own making.

Yet David's story doesn't end there.

In a world quick to cancel and discard those who fall, God's response to David is striking. Most of the psalms David wrote—those sacred words that have healed hearts for centuries—came after the Bathsheba incident. God didn't erase David's worst chapter. He inspired David to write through it and then for many more years thereafter. In a way that runs counter to our cultural instincts, God didn't bury David's shame or unleash a mob to bury and erase him. Instead he transformed him. He didn't scrub the record clean or parade David's failures for public scorn. He wove them into the larger story of redemption, one that would comfort the broken for generations and bequeath upon David the title of "man after God's own heart" and lead Jesus, the Mercy King, to refer to himself as "the Root and the Offspring of David" (1 Sam. 13:14; Rev. 22:16).

Perhaps this is the very scandal of grace: its refusal to flinch at our failures, and its insistence on redeeming our darkest, most humiliating chapters. Could it be that this grace—so radical, so unlike anything the world offers—is one of the strongest evidences for the truth of Christianity? Because what else explains a love that sees the worst and still draws near?

Like Zacchaeus we all carry reasons to believe we're beyond mercy. But the gospel insists otherwise. In Christ we are defined not by our worst and least lovable moments but by his best and most loving ones. Unlike every other religious system that divides the world into good and bad based on performance, the gospel turns the whole system upside down.

It doesn't reward self-effort.

It lavishes divine grace.

God's mercy flows not to the morally qualified but to the humble, to the ones who know they can't earn their way back. Grace is famously unsettling to those who believe they can. That's part of the ongoing criticism Christianity receives: If grace is real, why are some of its followers so disappointing? Critics point to hypocrisy, to centuries of missteps—the Crusades, politicized faith, moral failings, and cultural compromise. These critiques aren't new. And they aren't always unfair. But they also raise a deeper question: If we reject Christ because of the failures of his followers, is that fair to Christ himself?

Imagine attending a piano recital where a child fumbles through a Mozart piece, missing notes, losing the rhythm. Would we conclude that Mozart's music is overrated based on that flawed performance? Of course not.

In the same spirit, Russian novelist Leo Tolstoy, himself a deeply flawed believer, once wrote to a critic, "Attack me rather than the path I follow, in which I point out to anyone who asks me where I think the truth lies. If I know the way home and am walking along it drunkenly, is it any less the right way because I am staggering from side to side?"[2]

Tolstoy's retort echoes a deeper gospel truth: God is patient with our failures. His mercy remains when we stagger and stumble. The gospel doesn't depend on our consistency. It rests on Christ's.

While other religions and philosophies say, "Do good, keep the rules, and maybe you'll receive a reward," the Mercy King offers the opposite: "Here is your reward, already secured. Now, let's walk together and see who you become in light of it."

Grace comes first. It always comes first.

This is why people like Zacchaeus—the known sinners, the outcasts, the moral misfits—are drawn to Jesus in ways few others can understand. For those who know their need, grace falls like rain on parched soil. It heals. It transforms. It restores dignity to those the world has written off.

Just yesterday I had the privilege of visiting several men on death row. Many of them, having been pursued and loved by Christ in the midst of their darkest days, radiated a joy and serenity that would stir holy envy in many who've never spent a day behind bars or committed a crime.

One commented, "I hate what I did twenty-three years ago, and I feel sad that most people define my whole life by my worst five minutes. At the same time, I met Jesus behind these bars, and I am a different and eternally grateful man because of that."

A second man, whose death sentence has been lifted after spending thirty-seven years in prison for a crime he didn't commit—thanks to new and compelling forensic evidence uncovered by affiliates of the Innocence Project—said, "Some people call this death row, but I call it life row. The desperation I felt, knowing I might spend the rest of my life here and be executed for something I didn't do, is what brought me to Jesus."

There were many other comments like this. These men were the farthest thing from monsters. They were kind, humble, godly men who had, in the "worst five minutes of their lives," snapped and done an unthinkable thing. There was no pretense in the room, only the quiet freedom of men who knew they'd been forgiven much, and loved even more.

By contrast, for those convinced of their own goodness—for those who've built their identity around being the good ones—grace can feel like an offense. These "middle-class in spirit" souls often struggle to grasp the gospel, not because it's unclear but because they've never had to live at ground level, where repentance is real and where Jesus makes his home.

To meet Jesus, to really meet him, we must do something more than say our prayers and go to church. We must descend to the low place. We must come down. We must let go of the idea that we are owed or entitled to anything. We must release our moral résumés. There is no fee, and there is no option to pay our own way. The price of entry—the cover charge—is a humble heart and an empty set of hands.

It's here in the low place where grace and mercy reside. Where the proud can only suffocate and the broken find their breath again. It's here that the ones society has written off are warmly received and called the Mercy King's beloved.

If Jesus will receive a man like Zacchaeus in this way, it sends a strong message to the rest of us: Anyone, regardless of history or stature, can get in on this.

The Gift of a Good Name

For Zacchaeus, life was about to turn in a direction he never expected. A man who had built his career on exploiting others was now on the verge of an encounter that would change his life in every way. He had grown rich at the expense of his neighbors, trading connection for power and meaning for money. And yet for all his success, something in him still ached to be known, not as a villain but as a human being.

So he climbed a tree.

He didn't do it to make a scene. He did it because the crowd had no room for someone like him. Rejected and ignored he found a quiet place above the noise, just to catch a glimpse of Jesus. But Jesus didn't pass him by. He stopped, looked up, and called him by name. "Zacchaeus!" And with that simple act, the chief tax collector was both seen and welcomed.

This is the primal ache every heart carries: not only to be noticed but to be received.

Robin Williams once said, "I used to think the worst thing in life was to end up alone. It's not. The worst thing in life is to end up with people who make you feel alone."[3] His words echo an experience many of us know well: the quiet loneliness that lingers even in a room full of people. The kind of isolation that is solved not by presence but by connection.

Shame deepens that ache. It convinces us we are the sum of our failures, that our past disqualifies us from love. Over time we start to believe the lie that we are too far gone to belong. Brené Brown puts it this way: "A deep sense of love and belonging is an irreducible need of all people. We are biologically, cognitively, physically, and spiritually wired to love, to be loved, and to belong. When those needs are not met, we don't function as we were meant to. We break. We fall apart. We numb. We ache. We hurt others."[4]

Zacchaeus had spent years numbing that ache—through accumulation, through isolation, through denial. But the day Jesus saw him in that tree and called him by name, the ache was met with something far stronger: mercy.

Jesus didn't call him down for a lecture or a rebuke. He didn't ask for proof of repentance or remorse. He simply said, "Zacchaeus, come down. I'm coming to your house today." In Jesus' time, to enter someone's home was significant; it was a statement of friendship, an act of public acceptance. And he extended both to Zacchaeus before the man had done a single good thing.

This is how the gospel operates. We don't change to earn God's love. We change because we've been loved. We don't repent to gain his favor. We repent because his favor found us first. Zacchaeus didn't climb down the tree to earn something, he climbed down because something had already been given.

Whatever tree you're in today—whatever you've done, whatever rejection you've carried—Jesus sees you. And he's not waiting for a cleaner, tidier version of you to show up. He calls your name now, right where you are and just as you are. The Mercy King wants to turn your isolation into intimacy and replace your shame with welcome. Even if you struggle to believe this, your doubt makes it no less true.

From Taking to Giving

Zacchaeus's story doesn't end with a shared meal or a simple conversation. That single encounter with Jesus changed him from the inside out. The man once known for taking now became known for giving. The chief extortionist became a generous benefactor.

The Greek word for *grace*—*charis*—shares a root with *charity.* After receiving this unearned grace from Jesus, Zacchaeus became a living expression of it: openhanded, generous, and eager to make things right with all whom he had wronged. What once felt like a great cost now seemed like no cost at all. His new life wasn't just better. It was the only path he considered worth following.

Zacchaeus's transformation illustrates what happens when someone has an encounter with the Mercy King. At first, surrender may feel like obligation. But as Jesus becomes more real, obligation softens into desire, and desire into joy. What once was a "have to" becomes a "want to," then a glad "get to." Eventually, not following Jesus feels far more burdensome than following him.

Zacchaeus didn't just make promises, he acted with resolved follow-through. He gave half his possessions to the poor and offered fourfold restitution to anyone he had defrauded. The law required only double repayment, but Zacchaeus went farther. This wasn't penance. It was gratitude in motion, the fruit of mercy and grace already received.

Now this chief tax collector's home, once a symbol of exploitation, became a place of welcome. He could take the plastic off the furniture, let the fine wine and costly oil spill where they may, every stain a sign of something new. His wealth no longer served him. It served others. His life was now defined not by accumulation but by transformation, sealed by the mercy of a King who would soon hang from another tree to cover Zacchaeus in a far greater grace.

It is easy to imagine God as distant, distracted, or too busy for us. But if we could see what God is really up to, we would know beyond any doubt that he is pursuing us also. David knew this when he wrote, "Surely goodness and mercy shall follow me all the days of my life" (Ps. 23:6 ESV). That same mercy followed Zacchaeus. It called his name, entered his home, and remade his heart.

God's love doesn't separate the good from the bad. It reaches the outcast and the admired alike. Zacchaeus started the day small in stature, and even smaller in spirit. But by day's end he had been drawn into the vastness of God's mercy. Then what happened to the Grinch of Whoville also happened to Zacchaeus of Jericho: "His heart grew three sizes that day."[5]

Zacchaeus of Jericho thought he was looking for Jesus. But Jesus had been looking for him.

And he's looking for you too.

So what will you do when he calls your name?

Will you stay hidden in the branches, clinging to things that cannot save you? Or will you come down, open your heart and home, and follow the one whose mercy is deeper than your failures, stronger than your fears, and richer than anything this world can offer?

Come down.

Let him in.

And discover a mercy that will make you richer than cash and coin ever could.

Summary

Zacchaeus was known as a man of wealth, power, and exploitation, someone many viewed as beyond redemption. But in a surprising turn of grace, Jesus saw him differently. Without precondition Jesus extended mercy, calling Zacchaeus by name and offering not just a meal but belonging. That encounter changed everything. The chief taker became a joyful giver. In Zacchaeus's story we see the heart of Jesus, the Mercy King, who does not reward the deserving but pursues and restores the undeserving. Grace comes first. Always. And when received, it reshapes our identity, our relationships, and the way we live. What Jesus did for Zacchaeus, he still does today. The invitation remains open: Come down. Let him in. And discover a mercy richer than anything this world can offer.

Three Questions

1. Have you ever felt unseen, excluded, or defined by failures? What would it mean to believe that Jesus sees and calls you by name?
2. How does Jesus' scandalous grace challenge the way we think about merit, belonging, and usefulness in God's mission?
3. Who around you might be quietly longing for the kind of mercy Zacchaeus received? What would it look like for you to move toward them as Jesus did Zacchaeus?

One Action Step

This week pay attention to someone who may feel unseen or unworthy—perhaps a coworker, a neighbor, or even yourself. Find one way to reflect Jesus' mercy: Initiate a conversation, offer help without expectation, or speak a word of encouragement. Remember, Jesus calls people by name before they've proven anything—and so can we.

SEVEN

When Religion Beats You Down

The Mercy King Who Replaces Rules with Rest

> Jesus invites us to a new kind of rest: rest in God, rest that doesn't demand constant activity, but a deeper sense of security in being held by a love that doesn't depend on our performance.
>
> —Henri Nouwen, *The Way of the Heart*

In our fast-paced world, many of us carry a hidden burden—a persistent weariness, a restless ache that's hard to name. We keep up with schedules, meet our goals, and go through the motions of daily life, yet beneath it all runs an undercurrent of fatigue, a quiet sense that something isn't quite right.

The classic film *Chariots of Fire* offers a window into this very tension through the lives of two Olympic runners: Eric Liddell and

Harold Abrahams. Outwardly, they are nearly identical: young, gifted, and fiercely determined. But inwardly, they are running two very different races.

Liddell, a devoted Christian and future missionary to China, runs with an evident lightness, a peace that seems to come from beyond the track. In one of the film's most memorable scenes, his sister, Jennie, expresses concern that his athletic ambitions are distracting him from his missionary calling. Liddell's response reveals the quiet confidence and purpose that anchor him: "I believe that God made me for a purpose—for China. But he also made me fast. And when I run, I feel his pleasure." Throughout the story, Liddell embodies a joyful steadiness even as he trains and competes at the highest level.

By contrast Abrahams, a secular Jew, runs with equal passion, but without the same peace. In a moment of raw honesty, he confesses, "I have never known contentment. I'm forever in pursuit, and I don't even know what it is I'm chasing." He runs not for the joy of it but to prove himself. Though he and Liddell share the same track, their inner worlds could not be farther apart—one at rest, the other anxiously striving.[1]

This is more than a sports story, it's a mirror. Two runners, two ways of being in the world. One moves with freedom, knowing he is already loved. The other, driven by fear and longing, runs to earn the love he's never quite found. The contrast invites reflection: Who do we relate to more? Are we like Liddell—grounded in purpose, finding joy in our efforts? Or more like Abrahams—always pushing, never arriving, our hearts just a little out of breath? Depending on the day, the answer may change.

Maybe this is why God, in his mercy, commands us to rest. Not as a burdensome rule but as a life-giving rhythm. The fourth commandment is not a suggestion, it's a loving insistence that we pause, breathe, and remember who we are. Jesus, our Mercy King, echoes this in his tender invitation: "Come to me, all you who are weary and burdened, and I will give you rest" (Matt. 11:28). He uses his kingly authority not to control or constrain us but to lead us into wholeness. He knows that our souls, like our bodies, cannot thrive without stillness. His call to rest isn't earned, it's given. In his kindness he commands what will heal. In his wisdom he slows us down not to hinder us but to move us forward.

I know something of this restlessness firsthand. For years I've struggled with insomnia, pleading with God for deeper, more restorative sleep. After more than a decade, I'm beginning to wonder whether my sleeplessness has been connected to how much I've resembled Abrahams—driven, restless, and always on—more than I'd like to admit.

One moment brought this home in a way I won't forget. While on a family vacation, my sister-in-law took a photo of all of us gathered around the dinner table. Later I saw it on social media, where a family member had tagged me with the caption, "Put down your phone, mister." There I was, physically present yet mentally somewhere else, absorbed in a screen instead of the people right in front of me.

A friend once told me something his wife had said to him that stopped me in my tracks: "You're an extrovert with strangers, but an introvert with the people who love you most." I laughed, but not because it wasn't true. It hit uncomfortably close to home. Depending on the day, I can be fully present and engaged, or completely distracted and distant. I'm attentive, yes, but not always in the places that matter most. I'm always fully present, but I'm not always fully present *here*.

When I catch myself in these moments of restless distraction, I realize they're often symptoms of a deeper issue: my integrity slipping. I start making excuses for my fast, get-it-done pace, but deep down I know they're just that: excuses.

So I want to invite you to join me in an honest reflection. In a culture that idolizes hustle and measures worth by output, what is the source of our weariness? Why do so many of us, surrounded by comfort and convenience and leisure, still feel depleted? This isn't just about needing more sleep. It's about a soul-level fatigue that wears on our relationships, our joy, and our ability to be present with God and one another. Left unchecked this restlessness doesn't just shape our calendars. It shapes our very posture toward life.

The Source of Our Restlessness

Jesus' invitation to rest comes with a vivid image: a yoke. In his day a yoke was a heavy wooden harness that joined oxen together, enabling them to pull loads across fields. By choosing this metaphor Jesus reveals something universally true about our human experience:

We are all yoked to something.

All of us are carrying some kind of weight.

Into this reality the Mercy King steps not with more pressure but with a gracious invitation: "Take my yoke upon you . . . for my yoke is easy and my burden is light" (Matt. 11:29–30). He doesn't eliminate the idea of a yoke altogether, because life always comes with some weight we must carry. Instead he offers a yoke of grace, not performance; restoration, not depletion. To be yoked to Jesus is to be tethered to the gentlest strength, to walk in step with one who carries the heaviest load for us.

The real question, then, isn't whether we're yoked, but to what. Many of us are unknowingly burdened by harsh yokes: perfectionism that whispers "not enough," shame that replays decisions we wish we'd never made or actions we wish we hadn't taken, or anxiety that insists we hold everything together. These yokes take much from us and offer little in return.

And most of them? We've chosen freely.

Each of us has something we look to for our sense of worth, identity, or security. Archbishop William Temple once observed, "Your true religion is what you do with your solitude. It's where your mind goes when you have a moment of quiet."[2] So where does your mind wander when life finally slows? What hopes or fears show up most? What are the imagined disasters that play out at night?

For me, I have a recurring dream: I'm walking up to a podium to speak, only to realize I'm completely unprepared. I scramble for notes, searching for words as the seconds tick by—and then I wake up in a sweat. It's a dream that reveals something deeper: not just my desire to do well but my fear of disappointing others, of being found out, of being not enough. Some call it impostor syndrome.

It's a yoke I've placed on myself. And it's not light.

Heavy yokes take different forms for all of us. For some it's the pressure to look a certain way, leading to cycles of comparison, self-criticism, overexercising, and undereating. For others, it's the drive to succeed, to prove themselves through career or status, like Harold Abrahams in *Chariots of Fire*, who confesses he's "forever in pursuit," but unsure of what. Or Rocky Balboa, who just wants to "go the distance" to prove he's "not another bum."

Still others carry the quiet, exhausting burden of needing to be liked. When this happens, other people's approval becomes like emotional oxygen. Like a chameleon on a shifting canvas, some of us learn to blend in wherever we go—polishing our words, adjusting our tone and body language, curating a version of ourselves that feels most acceptable to the room we're in. One moment we speak fluent Christianese in a Bible study circle; the next we hide our convictions in the break room, locker room, or at a dinner party for fear of seeming too religious. It feels less like deceit and more like survival. We hope, often unconsciously, that if we can just be enough—charming enough, agreeable enough, likable enough—then maybe we won't be rejected. Maybe we'll finally feel safe.

This ache for approval doesn't stop at our relationships with others. It can also seep into our relationship with God. Instead of resting in grace, we perform for him, turning prayer and Scripture into duty-bound checklists. We forget that God's love isn't a reward for good behavior but a gift to savor and enjoy.

He's already told us so. The biblical story is one of creation, redemption, and hope—a promise that nothing can separate us from his love in Christ. This love is an invitation not only to receive him like a bride receives her groom but also to rest in his arms with quiet joy and freedom. Most rulers demand loyalty before love, obedience before affection, compliance as a condition for reward. But the Mercy King reverses the order: He loves first and invites us to respond, not to earn our spot.

Still we often fall back into striving. As Kathy Keller once put it, performance is "the natural religion of the human heart," a reflex to prove ourselves, even though Jesus already declared us worthy through his finished work.[3]

The prophet Isaiah speaks directly to this kind of weariness: "In repentance and rest is your salvation, in quietness and trust is your strength, but you would have none of it" (Isa. 30:15).

Beneath our striving lies a haunting litany of questions: "Am I loved? Do I matter? Will I still be accepted if I fail?"

To all of this, Jesus offers an invitation that sounds too good to be true: Lay down the yokes that tire us and take up his instead. Life with him is not about managing an image or striving for pats on the back. It's about being held. Being loved. Just as we are, right where we are.

Whether or not we consider ourselves religious, we each live under something that functions like law, an internal voice that says, "Prove yourself. Be enough. Be better. Do better." Jesus calls us out of that exhausting cycle. As King he doesn't say, "Impress me." He says, "Come to me and rest."

Be loved. Be forgiven. Be free.

His authority makes his mercy both possible and accessible.

He's not a ruler who exploits our weakness. He's a King who bears our burdens. He doesn't demand that we bring our best foot forward everywhere, all the time. He offers rest and renewal when all we can do is put our worst foot forward.

Rest for the Weary

In Matthew's gospel Jesus offers a remedy for anxious souls who struggle to find rest. He invites us to bring all our burdens—those pursuits we chase for validation, security, or significance—and exchange them for his yoke, which he describes as easy, and his burden, which is light (Matt. 11:28–30).

Jesus doesn't approach us as a harsh taskmaster, pointing out flaws or keeping score. Instead his invitation is tender and personal: "Come to me, all who are weary, and I will give you rest." This call isn't toward a program, a religious practice, or even church attendance or a small group Bible study, though those can be helpful. It's an invitation to a person.

"Come to *me*." These three words are everything. Every spiritual practice—whether prayer, reading Scripture, worship, or service—is ultimately meant to draw us into a relationship with Jesus himself. When we lose sight of that, even the most admirable and meaningful rhythms can become burdensome, leaving us with a vague sense of guilt and not-enoughness.

What Jesus offers is what every other pursuit promises but cannot deliver. Careers, achievements, and affirmation for a job well done often hold out the illusion of significance and fulfillment, because they speak to real, God-given desires to matter, to be seen, and to have purpose. But when these good things become ultimate things, they turn into fragile foundations. They rise and fall with our performance, the opinions of others, or circumstances we can't control. And in the end they leave us anxious, insecure, and wanting. Jesus, by contrast, says, "You are already known. Already loved. Already secure."

In him our identity is established, so we're free to engage in meaningful, productive endeavors not as ways to prove our worth but as ways to live out our belovedness. When we know we are loved in both our best and worst moments, we move through life with greater confidence, joy, and lightness of being. We no longer need to win approval to feel like we matter.

For those of us who, like Woody Allen's character Leonard Zelig, are tempted to shape-shift to be accepted, Jesus offers a far better way. In the film, Zelig becomes whoever he needs to be to fit in: transforming into a kindly nun when surrounded by nuns, and adopting the mannerisms of a fascist when in the company of dictators. His identity is always in flux, molded by the crowd, driven by the fear of rejection. But time and again Jesus reminds us we are already beloved. Already treasured. We don't need to chase belonging. In him we are already home. Scripture describes us as "the apple of his eye," cherished sons and daughters in whom he delights. He rejoices over us with gladness, quiets us with his love, and sings over us with joy (Zeph. 3:17).

Nothing—not our deepest regrets, our darkest fears, or our worst failures—can separate us from that love (Rom. 8:38–39). The same King who left the ninety-nine to find the one calls us now not to contribute more, not to shape up or ship out, but to rest. The maker of stars and galaxies can't love us more than he already does. Nor is he capable of loving us any less.

What could be more comforting than that?

"I will give you rest." This is more than an offer of escape from a busy week. Jesus is promising deep, soul-level renewal—a sabbath rest that touches every real or potentially worn-out, burned-out corner of our lives. From the beginning this rest has been woven into creation itself: six days of work followed by one day for reflection and renewal. Sabbath isn't a luxury, it's a declaration. A way of saying, "God is enough. His provision is enough. I don't have to carry everything."

And it's not just about taking a day off. Sabbath is a posture of trust. A rhythm of receiving. A resistance against the hurried, hyperefficient pace of modern life. Like deep, restorative sleep, Sabbath refreshes us not only physically but spiritually, emotionally, and relationally.

Studies on sleep have shown that quality often matters even more than quantity. A few hours of deep rest can restore more than an entire night of tossing and turning. In the same way, a few unhurried moments with Jesus can ground us for the whole day. His rest isn't a break from real life, it's what makes real life meaningful and sustainable. "My yoke is easy," he says, "and my burden is light."

To live into this promise, we need rhythms that pull us out of the anxious cycles that consume us. This includes regular worship, meaningful connection with others, life-giving spiritual reading and teaching, and rest—true breaks when we unplug and recharge. Author and theologian Walter Brueggemann calls this "detaching from the anxiety system of Pharaoh."[4]

In Exodus, Pharaoh forced the Israelites to make bricks without straw. Today we each carry an inner Pharaoh, a voice that pushes us to produce more, prove more, and earn more. Brueggemann suggests that Sabbath is our rebellion against this pressure. It's how we remind ourselves that our value isn't tied to our performance.

As it has been said, "Almost everything will work again if you unplug it, including you."[5]

But Sabbath isn't only about rhythms, it's about trust. Why is it so hard to stop striving? Why do we keep picking up burdens that Jesus has already carried? Rest doesn't begin with a schedule change, it begins with surrender.

Until we believe Jesus is enough, we will keep running.

Real rest starts with trust—trust that his love really is unconditional and undemanding, that his grace really is sufficient and safe, and that his generous invitation really does extend to people like us.

"Take my yoke upon you." When Jesus extends this invitation, he redefines rest not as the absence of work but as an act of receiving. To take his yoke is to choose to step away from the world's frantic pace and cultivate rhythms of retreat, stillness, and solitude. Just as we schedule time for meals or commit to showing up at work, rest is not optional for a flourishing life. It's essential.

Even major companies are beginning to understand this. For years Google has topped *Fortune*'s list of Top 100 Companies to Work For. Known for extraordinary productivity, Google also prioritizes rest. Employees are offered generous vacation time, extended parental leave, and even nap pods in the office. The company expects excellence but understands that rest fuels creativity, morale, and long-term performance. Their approach demonstrates our point: Most things, especially people, function best when allowed to pause, breathe, and renew.

Another high performer and a former Twitter executive, Claire Diaz-Ortiz, wrote an entire book on accomplishing more by working less. Her philosophy centers on working smarter, not harder, built on an uncompromising foundation of rest. Far from equating rest with laziness, she reframes it as wisdom—a balanced way of living that acknowledges our limitations and releases the illusion of control. In this way rest becomes an act of faith, a declaration that stepping back can be more fruitful than pushing through.[6]

At the heart of Sabbath is this kind of trust. Whether it's our time, our finances, or our personal and professional goals, the areas in which God asks us to surrender often reveal how much we actually trust him. Take, for instance, the biblical call to give 10 percent of our income. When that feels impossible, it's often not just a budgeting challenge, it's a trust issue. Do we really believe that God can meet 100 percent of our needs with less than 100 percent of our resources? Or are we clinging to the myth of self-sufficiency?

Sabbath works the same way with our time. God invites us to set aside one full day—one seventh of our week—as a sacred pause. And in return he promises seven days of provision out of six days of labor. It's as if he says, "Trust me. You'll flourish and even produce more, over the course of time, when you strive less."

This invitation to rest was especially countercultural for ancient Israel. Even during the harvest season—the busiest and most critical time of their year—God called his people to pause, to rest, and to trust him. He reinforced this rhythm of trust in the wilderness through the daily provision of manna—a sweet, flaky bread that appeared each morning like dew on the ground. The Israelites were instructed to gather only enough for that day and to refrain from collecting any on the Sabbath. When some tried to gather extra, the manna spoiled, an unforgettable lesson that God's provision can't be hoarded and that grace comes fresh each day.

Six days of work.

One day of trust.

And yet seven days of provision.

But Sabbath isn't the only way Jesus offers rest. He also invites us into the daily means of grace: simple, consistent moments of connection with him. Just as small gestures sustain a deep friendship, even fifteen to thirty minutes each day with God—through Scripture, prayer, or quiet reflection—can reset our perspective and steady our hearts.

Charles Spurgeon, famously known as the "Prince of Preachers," battled anxiety, insomnia, and depression throughout his life. Yet he once said, "A Bible that is falling apart usually belongs to someone who isn't."[7] He understood that a regular connection with God is a steadying force, even in seasons of inner restlessness.

When Jesus says, "Take my yoke," he's not asking us to carry more. He's inviting us to carry less. His yoke doesn't demand that we prove ourselves or keep up appearances. Instead it frees us to rely on his strength, to release the burdens that leave us feeling small, anxious, or tired.

This yoke is gentle. His heart is kind. And when we receive what he offers, we discover a rest that renews us in ways nothing else can. Not just rest from work but rest from worry. Not just rest for the body but deep slumber for the soul.

How We Enter His Rest

Jesus' invitation to rest isn't just a promise of relief, it's a call to adopt the posture of a trusting child. Just before he speaks of his easy yoke and light burden, Jesus thanks the Father for revealing these things "to little children" (Matt. 11:25–27).

That phrase—"little children"—is rich with meaning. It evokes openness, humility, playfulness, and dependence. Jesus is inviting us to a way of being in which we receive his love, rest in his care, and live free from the pressure to shoulder life's weight alone.

Think about how children live. Their role is simple: to be loved, to be cared for, to eat, to sleep, to play. Their role in life is to receive. When children feel safe and secure, they move through the day in confidence. They laugh easily, sleep deeply, and live fully in the moment—without carrying tomorrow's worries. Watching children at play, you may have found yourself thinking, "Wouldn't it be something to live like that again?"

That's exactly what Jesus is inviting us to.

"Live like *that*," he says. "Become a child again."

Children live freely because they trust that the weight of the world is not on their shoulders. They assume—rightly—that someone else, someone stronger and more capable, is carrying the load. When fear, conflict, or uncertainty strikes, they run to the ones who love them most, trusting those arms to hold them together.

I remember when our daughters were young and would wake in the night, scared or unsettled. They would come to us, seeking comfort, and all it took was wrapping them in our arms. Every time, they would fall asleep again, secure in love, wrapped in protection, surrounded with care.

That's the kind of safety Jesus offers. Regardless of our age, our pressures, or the roles we carry—whether we're children or parents, CEOs or students, with wind at our backs or wind in our faces—Jesus invites us to release the burdens we were never meant to carry and entrust them to him, the Mercy King. Unlike earthly parents, who grow tired or distracted, our Lord never slumbers, never steps away, never grows weary of holding us.

Psalm 121 reminds us that the Lord "will neither slumber nor sleep. The LORD watches over you—the LORD is your shade at your right hand." His care is constant. His love is unwavering. He doesn't let go.

But how can we trust that God will stay with us, especially in our darkest moments? The answer is Jesus.

On the night before the cross, Jesus experienced the ultimate restlessness. His soul was, in his own words, "overwhelmed with sorrow to the point of death" (Matt. 26:38). The weight of the world's sin and sorrow crushed him to the point that he sweat drops of blood. He asked the Father if there was another way, but he chose surrender and submission. He bore our pain, our striving, and our exhaustion. And he did it alone. While his disciples slept, Jesus stayed awake so that we, in him, could finally rest.

At the cross, Jesus took on the heaviest burden of all. With his final breath he declared, "It is finished." In that moment, he moved our judgment day from the future to the past, securing our salvation and freedom. His work was complete, and it became the foundation of our peace. He also cried, "I thirst," so that we would never thirst again. In him we're grafted onto the family of God, carried by the one who bore every burden we'll ever face.

His body and blood, given for us, assure us that we are safe. Redeemed. Free. No more striving to earn worth, no more proving ourselves, no more running while not knowing what it is we are running for; Jesus has already declared our value. Because of this, what once felt like duty now becomes delight. What was once an unreachable goal becomes a gift. The things we once believed we had to do become things we get to do.

One old hymn says it well:

> To see the Law of Christ fulfilled,
> to hear his pardoning voice,
> turns a slave into a child,
> and duty into choice.[8]

If Jesus has already carried our greatest burden, why do we still insist on carrying the smaller ones alone? This is why he invites us—pleads with us—to let go.

So come, all who are weary. You don't have to live under this weight anymore. The world will always tell you that rest must be earned, that love must be proven. But Jesus says the work is done. The burden is lifted. Your worth is secure.

The question now is this: Will you keep striving, or will you surrender?

Will you keep running, or will you finally rest?

His arms are open. His invitation still stands. Lay down your burdens. Step into the rest of Jesus not just for a moment or for an hour on Sunday but for the rest of your days.

Summary

In a world that glorifies hustle and measures worth by performance, Jesus offers something radically different: rest. Not merely physical rest but soul-level renewal that comes from being tethered to the Mercy King, who carries our heaviest burdens. His easy yoke frees us from the wearying cycles of perfectionism, approval seeking, and self-reliance. Rooted in grace, not performance, this rest reorients our identity around what is already true and can't be changed: We are known, loved, and secure in him. The invitation isn't to do more but to trust more. To stop shape-shifting for acceptance and instead live as beloved children, grounded in the steady love of the one who never sleeps, never lets go, and never asks us to earn what he has already given.

Three Questions

1. What are the heavy yokes—expectations, pressures, or internal voices—you've been carrying that Jesus is inviting you to lay down?
2. When you imagine Jesus saying, "Come to me, and I will give you rest," what part of your life most needs to receive that invitation today?
3. Where might you be shape-shifting like Zelig—adjusting who you are to feel accepted—and how does Jesus' love offer you a more secure identity?

One Action Step

This week set aside one Sabbath window—whether an hour, an afternoon, or a full day. Unplug. Turn off notifications. Instead of producing or performing, simply rest in God's presence. Let your actions say, "I trust you to hold my world while I rest." Whether through quiet prayer, a walk, journaling, or stillness, let this time be a lived expression of your trust in the Mercy King.

EIGHT

When Ruthless Trust Is Your Only Option

The Mercy King Who Makes Ordinary People Brave

> Faith is taking the first step even when you don't see the whole staircase.
>
> —Martin Luther King Jr., *Strength to Love*

Now I'd like to turn our focus to Mary, the virgin mother of Jesus, a valiant teenage woman whose story inspires awe in some and stirs hard questions in others.

Faith often begins in tension. Perhaps you've felt it too, that moment when what you know collides with what seems impossible. Trusting God in suffering. Believing he is good even when life doesn't feel that way. Holding onto his promises when evidence whispers otherwise. Mary's story enters this same space—the struggle between belief and uncertainty—as she becomes pregnant not by a man but by the Holy Spirit.

It's often in the thick of mystery that the character of the Mercy King is revealed. God's mercy doesn't wait for our clarity; it meets us in confusion, hesitation, and honest questions. In Mary's surrender we glimpse the heart of the son she would cradle: He comes gently, humbly, and impossibly close, not standing over our doubts but stepping into them, carrying mercy in one hand and invitation in the other.

Can we trust the impossible—that God's ways are higher than ours? Mary's story isn't just doctrine to affirm, it's a call to journey from uncertainty to trust.

Imagine being Mary. A teenager, visited by an angel with words that would reshape her entire life. Would Joseph believe her? Would her parents reject her? Would her community shame her? The weight of uncertainty pressed in, and she had every reason to ask, "How can this be? Why me? What will this cost?"

Yet somehow in the midst of the unknown, Mary arrived at quiet surrender: "Let it be to me according to your word" (Luke 1:38 ESV). This wasn't resignation. It was gut-level faith, a trust so deep she staked her entire future on a promise from God, and nothing more.

What's striking is not only the boldness of this moment but the tenderness. Mary's response invites us to consider our own stories. Have you ever stood at the edge of the unknown, where obedience means risk and trust guarantees sacrifice? Her story reminds us that faith is not the absence of fear and doubt but the presence of trust and obedience amid them.

While unique in its own right, Mary's journey also feels familiar. We too are asked to believe when answers are elusive, to trust in God's goodness when everything feels uncertain and shaky.

It's here that the Mercy King's heart is once again revealed.

Faith is not about having all the answers, it's about trusting the one who does. Jesus, the Mercy King, never separates his commands from his care. He is not just a comforter in our doubts. He is a royal who invites what Brennan Manning calls "ruthless trust."[1]

With the King's call to ruthless trust in mind, let's turn more fully to Mary. Like so many who have walked the road of belief, she had to move through a series of questions to arrive at trust. We'll explore her journey in two parts: first how doubt, far from being an enemy of faith, can actually strengthen it; and second how a maturing faith brings the peace of surrender.

Mary, the Mercy King's mother, invites us to bring our honest questions to God not as a barrier to faith but as a pathway through which trust is born.

The Virtue of Doubt

Let's start with doubt.

Doubt isn't the opposite of faith. Unbelief is. It can actually be a vital step on the journey to more settled, confident conviction. For many faith deepens not in the absence of questions but through them. Some people come to believe in Jesus naturally, with little internal wrestling. Perhaps they grew up in homes where faith was simply part of life—creeds, confessions, and Scripture recited on Sundays, trust in Jesus woven into daily rhythms. Trust in God's promises for them came naturally, almost effortlessly.

That may even describe Joseph, Mary's fiancé. When the angel appeared to him and said, "Do not be afraid . . . you will name the child Jesus," Joseph simply got up and did what the Lord commanded. No recorded hesitation. No signs of inner turmoil.

Mary, on the other hand, responded differently. When given what appears to be the same message, perhaps even from the same angel, her immediate reaction was shock, awe, and questioning. We're told she was "greatly troubled" and asked, "How will this be, since I am a virgin?" (Luke 1:29, 34).

Her biological reality alone raised obvious questions. But her doubt ran deeper than that. It also carried social, cultural, theological, and emotional weight.

Mary had every reason to hesitate. She was a poor girl from an obscure town, asked to carry a message so audacious it bordered on the absurd. "Can anything good come out of Nazareth?" The whispers of doubt likely came not just from her village but from within her own heart. "Who am I to carry God's Son? Of all the women in the world, why would God choose me?"

But isn't that how faith often feels? As if we are too ordinary, too unqualified, too random to be called into something extraordinary?

We, too, struggle to believe that God notices us when we feel invisible, that he has a plan when life feels out of control or that he's close by when we feel forgotten. But Mary's story is our story too. The Mercy King delights in empowering unlikely vessels. If God were going to make a world-shaking announcement, most would expect it to happen in Jerusalem—the religious and cultural heart of Jewish life. But instead the message arrives in a forgotten corner of the map. A place more akin to the Rust Belt than a royal court. Unimpressive. Unremarkable. And yet that's exactly where God shows up, initiates, and moves his plan forward.

Consider also how this message would have landed on a devout Jew like Mary. In her tradition, God was infinitely holy—set apart, unreachable, even unspeakable. His name was considered too sacred to say aloud, often written in the Hebrew equivalent of *YHWH*, with vowels removed. For someone raised with that level of reverence, the idea that this same God would himself become a child—fragile, dependent, and nestled in the humble Mary's womb—was not just staggering. To many it would have sounded blasphemous.

Mary's age, too, underscored the strangeness of it all. Girls were typically betrothed around twelve or fourteen. In today's terms she would've just been old enough to start attending a church youth group. And yet at this young age she was handpicked by God to carry, protect, and raise his only begotten Son. A message this weighty would more logically be entrusted to a respected rabbi, not an unknown teenager at the dawn of adulthood.

Mary's social status added yet another layer of improbability. Later in Luke's gospel we learn that when she and Joseph bring Jesus to the temple, they offer a pair of birds—the offering permitted for those too poor to afford a lamb. It's where we get the "two turtle doves" from the holiday carol. Mary came from poverty. From obscurity. From the margins.

There was also her gender. In Mary's world, women's voices were often dismissed. Their testimonies weren't admissible in court. Society viewed them as unreliable witnesses, limited in both voice and influence. And yet in his gospel, Luke goes out of his way to spotlight women—including Mary, Mary Magdalene, Joanna, plus others—as central to Jesus' story. The apostle Paul does the same at the close of several of his letters, placing women on the same level as men concerning their dignity, their place in God's kingdom, and their capacity to serve and lead. It was women who stayed at the cross when others fled in fear. Women were the first to witness the resurrection. Women were the first to tell the good news that Christ had risen, becoming apostles to the apostles.

In that light, Mary's being chosen as the *Theotokos*—the Greek term meaning "God-bearer"—becomes all the more radical. Today, we rightly affirm and champion the equal dignity of men and women as image-bearers of God. But in Mary's time such equality would have been shocking, even offensive. As C. S. Lewis once remarked, Christianity must be true—because no one would have made it up this way.[2] No one in those days invents a story in which the fate of the world rests on the faith of a young, invisible girl from Nazareth.

If you find yourself skeptical, take heart: The gospel of Luke—and the whole of Scripture—invites your honest questions. It doesn't sanitize the doubts of its key figures, such as Mary. Instead it honors them. The church at its best will carry forward this tradition, creating space for curiosity, for struggle, for the kind of faith that wrestles before it settles in. After all, where better to wrestle with the impossible than in the presence of a God who *does* the impossible?

Mary's story reminds us that faith rarely grows in the absence of doubt. It often flourishes right in the thick of it. Abraham questioned. Moses hesitated. Thomas demanded proof. And in each case, the Mercy King met them not with a pointed finger but with evidence intertwined with care.

The Mercy King, who sought out sinners in their brokenness, also sought Mary in her virtue. Before she reached for him, he was already reaching for her. He reaches in the same way for us.

Ruthless trust doesn't mean having every answer.

It means trusting the one who *is* the answer.

To the Thinking Skeptic

If you're skeptical about Christianity because of its miracles—whether it's the virgin birth, the parting of the Red Sea, manna from the sky, or Jesus healing the blind, turning water into wine, and rising from the dead—consider this: dismissing the entire Christian story simply because it includes miracles may not be as rational as it seems.

Many reject stories like the virgin birth on the grounds that they aren't scientifically plausible, without looking any closer. But do we apply that same scrutiny to scientific theories that also defy logic?

Take, for example, the idea that the universe and all life within it emerged without a creator. The complexity of human existence—from fingerprints and lungs to memory, consciousness, and love—is staggering. And yet many who don't believe in God turn to evolutionary theory to explain it all, despite how statistically improbable certain aspects of Darwinism may be.

I once asked a prominent scientist how he navigates conversations about his Christian faith—particularly his belief in the Genesis creation narrative—with skeptical colleagues. His response was refreshingly candid. "Let's assume," he would say, "that evolutionary theory is completely accurate—that everything from stars and planets to ecosystems and humanity came into being on its own, without any other first cause. Even then we must admit the outcome is extraordinarily unlikely. If life emerged purely by chance, that's a kind of miracle in itself, a leap of faith that might even be greater than belief in a creator who designed it all."

Whether one believes the universe emerged all by itself or was created by a personal God, both positions require faith. Neither belief nor unbelief can be proven beyond all doubt. In that way, we all stand on level ground.

To the Honest Doubter

If you wrestle with doubt, Mary's story—and God's response to her questions—offers encouragement.

Don't be pressured into burying your questions and doubts. Sometimes when people say, "Just believe it. The Bible says so, therefore deal with it," what they're really expressing is fear. Fear that something deeply precious to them might not become precious to you. Fear that your questions could shake the foundation of their own faith. But God's truth doesn't ask us to guard and protect it. It's strong enough to handle our doubts, sturdy enough to hold up under scrutiny. God often draws us closer not in spite of our questions but through them. Honest engagement isn't a threat to faith. It's often the soil where deeper trust grows.

In Mary's case, her response was not passive acceptance but thoughtful inquiry: "How will this be, since I am a virgin?" The Greek word used here suggests reasoning, pondering, even dialoguing. Her open mind wasn't a threat to her faith, it was the path that led her there.

Of course, doubt is never meant to be a permanent destination. It's a bridge meant to lead somewhere—to clarity, to conviction, to trust. Staying in doubt indefinitely can leave us stuck, even cynical. Sometimes rejecting the Bible by pointing out apparent contradictions is more about sidestepping its claims than engaging with them. The Bible doesn't just offer meaningful answers, it also poses hard questions. It confronts us more than we confront it—challenging our assumptions, exposing our sins and scars, and calling us to something higher.

Sometimes those who walk away from Christianity are rejecting it not because of intellectual objections but because of emotional or experiential ones. Some feel upset with a God they claim not to believe in, a tension that often signals a deeper longing beneath the doubt.

This isn't to shame those who question but to honor the difference between healthy doubt and disingenuous dismissal. Healthy doubt asks hard questions and lingers long enough to seek real answers. It's not afraid to dig. And it's willing to arrive at a thoughtful conclusion, even if that conclusion is unexpected.

Many public intellectuals have made that journey. Os Guinness, a scholar who once questioned the claims of Christianity, said that while doubt is normal, it is meant to be temporary, a way station on the road to clarity.[3] G. K. Chesterton famously observed, "The purpose of an open mind is the same as that of an open mouth—to shut it on something solid."[4]

God didn't leave Mary alone in her questions. He gave her the Holy Spirit, who opens hearts to believe what might otherwise seem impossible. The Spirit is God's very presence—alive, personal, empowering belief.

God also gave Mary reassurance in the form of Elizabeth, her older relative, who, though long past childbearing age, was miraculously pregnant with John the Baptist. Through Elizabeth's pregnancy, God was saying to Mary, "Here's something you can see to help you settle in with my promise to do the impossible in and through you. It is true that apart from me, you can do nothing. It is also true that with me, *nothing* is impossible."

As the Creator, God isn't constrained by the systems he designed. He can work within natural laws—or transcend and override them—for his purposes and our good. As Francis Schaeffer once said, God "is there, and he is not silent."[5]

Mary's journey shows what it looks like when faith takes root through the avenues of doubt. A young girl from a forgotten town, faced with an unthinkable call, questioned, listened, pondered—and ultimately said a surrendered yes: "Behold, I am the servant of the Lord. Let it be to me according to your word."

The Cost and Blessings of Ruthless Trust

Healthy doubt can be a bridge to deeper conviction. But for Mary it also required her to step into a journey marked by both profound joy and deep sorrow.

When the angel Gabriel announced to her, "You will bear a son," he was inviting her into a calling that would upend her life physically, emotionally, and socially. Saying yes meant far more than consenting to pregnancy. The journey she agreed to embark on would cost her more than she or Joseph could possibly imagine.

By accepting her role in the carrying, birthing, and raising of the Mercy King, Mary subjected herself to a ripple effect of merciless consequences. Her yes to God exposed her to suspicion, gossip, and rejection from family and community alike. People would notice the timing. She'd be visibly pregnant on her wedding day, and the whispers would begin. The math wouldn't add up. To many she would become the carrier of a scarlet letter, a subject of gossip and an object of judgment and shame.

The weight of that gossip and shame wouldn't fall on her alone. It would ripple outward to her family, and especially to her son. Jesus would grow up under the cloud of controversy. As a child he would confound his parents by disappearing for days, staying behind in the temple with the rabbis. Mary would know the worry and frustration of a parent searching for a missing child. But this would be only the beginning of her grief.

As a young adult, Jesus would provoke strong, divided reactions. His teachings would comfort the brokenhearted and confront the powerful. He would be too radical for some, too traditional for others, and unsettling for nearly everyone. Religious leaders would accuse him. Roman authorities would fear him. Even those closest to Mary would pressure her to intervene, urging her to bring him back into line, to quiet the young man who stirred up so much trouble.

And then the deepest pain of all: the heartbreak of not being able to protect her child. Mary would become a widow, raising her family in Joseph's absence. And one day she would stand at the foot of a Roman cross, watching her son suffer and die a brutal death, a moment that would tear her heart in two.

The only mercy Mary would receive in that moment came from her dying son. From the cross, Jesus looked at her and said, "Woman, here is your son," and to John, the beloved disciple beside her, "Here is your mother" (John 19:26–27). From that moment on, we're told, John took Mary into his home. It's just like God—just like the Mercy King—that even in the midst of his agony and abandonment, he made sure his mother would not be left alone. He provided her with the mercy she would need not only to survive this cruel and crushing moment but to endure the long road ahead. I've often wondered why John, unlike the other disciples, wasn't martyred in his youth. My best guess is that Jesus, sovereign over all things, spared John so that Mary would have someone to walk with her, to care for her, to be family to her in the wake of his departure. Even from the grave—and later from the right hand of the Father—the mercy of Mary's son followed her all the days of her life.

Mary's faithful readiness to tether her life to the Mercy King—to carry him, raise him, and ultimately grieve him—reveals a deep, ruthless trust. It's the kind that says yes to God even when the road ahead is dire, and when saying yes means forfeiting all certainty, comfort, and reputation. Hers was a faith brave enough to embrace a future she couldn't predict, and tender enough to remain open to God, even when it would cost her—and him—everything.

Mary's yes to God is extraordinary because she gives it without knowing how the story will unfold. She doesn't ask for guarantees or demand a road map. She simply receives the one assurance Gabriel offers: "You are highly favored." For her that is enough. On the strength of that promise, Mary surrenders to God's mysterious vision for her life.

Hopeful Songs from Dire Places

But she doesn't quietly walk away from this encounter. Instead she breaks into song. The Magnificat—a poetic outpouring of joy and awe—still echoes today with beauty and boldness. What inspires her wonder? It's the realization that she's been chosen to participate with God in something miraculous, something beyond comprehension.

"He who is mighty has done great things for me," she marvels.

But what about us? None of us has experienced or witnessed a virgin birth. How do we fit into this story, centuries later?

Episcopal priest and author Fleming Rutledge offers insight here. In her Advent reflections, she reminds us that the same Holy Spirit who filled Mary also lives in everyone who believes. The promises that shaped Mary's story still hold true for ours. The Mighty One can do great things in our lives too—quiet, transformative miracles that begin from the inside out.

Rutledge highlights something striking about Mary's example: her no to her own plans and her yes to God's better, though more difficult, vision. And this too is where our participation in the story begins. Saying no to our own way in order to say yes to God's doesn't always look dramatic. Most of the time, the godward drama of our lives unfolds in the theater of the ordinary. Rutledge writes:

> The Christian life means participating in the struggle where the forces of evil are confronted by the power of God. This takes place not only in great and heroic acts, but in countless small decisions: to tell the truth when a lie would be easier; to stay faithful when it would be easier to walk away; to choose patience instead of anger, forgiveness instead of bitterness, hope instead of despair. These are not just moral choices—they are battlefronts in the ongoing war between the powers of Sin and the lordship of Jesus Christ.[6]

Put another way, faith is the avenue for joining God in his redemptive work—in big and seemingly small ways—even when it disrupts our plans and defies our impulses. Each act of faith, however grand or quiet, bears witness to the presence and movement of Jesus, a subtle yet real continuation of the miracle of his coming.

Just as Mary carried the promise of God within her, so do we. She bore Christ in her body; we bear the fruit of his Spirit in our lives. In a world that is often cold, divided, and hostile, we're empowered to bring forth "love, joy, peace, patience, kindness, goodness, faithfulness, gentleness, and self-control" (Gal. 5:22–23 ESV). When we live this way, we offer the world a more radiant, life-giving picture of humanity as God intends it.

Are you ready to give birth to that kind of miracle? Are you prepared to invite God's vision for your life to take root, even if it disrupts your lesser versions of the good life? The miracle of "Christ in you, the hope of glory" (Col. 1:27)—his life and love—is waiting to be conceived by the Holy Spirit, then birthed, and then revealed in and through you. The name Jesus means "he will save his people from their sins," and he is still doing that, by the billions.

In my own life, he took a young man who was selfish, afraid, and aimless and put him on a new path. Since Jesus came into my life, everything has changed. Just as it did for Mary.

I wouldn't trade it for anything.

How about you?

Jesus Will Ask You to Do Hard Things

Saying yes to the Mercy King often means stepping away from old patterns and embracing difficult, costly obedience. When I became a Christian, his call to deny myself, take up my cross, and follow him pressed me to reimagine what "the good life" really means.

God's first assignments to me, as someone who had long cared deeply about his own reputation, were unmistakably clear: confess and repair.

I had stolen a pair of athletic shorts from an employer, and the Spirit pressed on me to make it right—to admit the wrongdoing, return what I had taken, and accept whatever followed. I had also cheated on several college exams, claiming grades I hadn't truly earned and setting myself up to live a lie. Admitting this would also endanger a rare award I had received, given to only two men in my graduating class for character, honor, and integrity. Yet again the Spirit urged me toward honesty. I knew what needed to happen: I needed to contact the university president, confess everything, and be ready for the consequences. Either situation could have ended badly—legal trouble, loss of my degree, or loss of future opportunities. But that wasn't the point.

The point was this: The arrival of the Mercy King in my life, and the presence of his Spirit within me, gave me no choice but to bring my private life into alignment with my public one. I was being called to repair what I had broken, as best I could, and to begin walking a path of fuller integrity. It was the first step in a long journey toward becoming more like Christ by being *with* Christ and abiding *in* Christ.

And this, too, is a miracle: the quiet, internal transformation of a human heart by God's grace. Christ in us, Christ with us, shaping lives that reflect his love, humility, and character. Like Mary each of us can say, "Let it be to me according to your word," and become living witnesses of the Mercy King.

Mary's Prayer of Surrender

After her encounter with the angel—and her journey from honest doubt to faithful surrender—Mary responds not with pushback or hesitation but with worship. Her song, recorded in Luke's gospel (1:46–55) and known as the Magnificat, is more than a personal reflection. It is a bold proclamation of who God is, what he is like, and how he works in the world. Like a psalm, Mary's song gives us language for our own prayers. It praises God for his mercy, his justice, his faithfulness. In it we see the God-bearer fully embracing the cost of her calling with both humility and courage.

In her obedience Mary gives us access to the heart of her son. Jesus too would say yes to a mission that would cost him everything. Born into scandal and suffering, the Mercy King would wear a crown made not of gold but of thorns.

As for Mary's surrendered prayer, it has echoed through generations, bearing witness to a God who upends the world's values and elevates the meek and lowly. Her voice still invites us to believe that God's mercy reaches, especially, those the world tends to forget.

Let's read her song slowly now, allowing it to settle deep into our hearts:

> My soul glorifies the Lord
>   and my spirit rejoices in God my Savior,
> for he has been mindful
>   of the humble state of his servant.
> From now on all generations will call me blessed,
>   for the Mighty One has done great things for me—
>   holy is his name.
> His mercy extends to those who fear him,
>   from generation to generation.
> He has performed mighty deeds with his arm;
>   he has scattered those who are proud in their inmost thoughts.
> He has brought down rulers from their thrones
>   but has lifted up the humble.
> He has filled the hungry with good things
>   but has sent the rich away empty.
> He has helped his servant Israel,
>   remembering to be merciful
> to Abraham and his descendants forever,
>   just as he promised our ancestors.

Amen.

Summary

Mary's story shows us that faith doesn't begin with certainty, it begins with surrender. Her journey from honest doubt to wholehearted trust reflects the kind of ruthless trust that Jesus, the Mercy King, calls each of us into. Mary didn't demand proof or a clear path. She responded to mystery with a courageous yes, even when it meant shame, cost, and heartbreak. In doing so she became the first to carry Christ and a model for anyone invited into the costly joy of obedience. Her life reminds us that true faith is not the absence of questions but the presence of trust in the one who holds the answers. Like Mary we are invited to say, "Let it be to me according to your word," and to live lives shaped not by fear or control but by faith in the one whose mercy reigns.

Three Questions

1. Where in your life are you being asked to say yes to God, even when the cost feels high or the outcome unclear?
2. How does Mary's trust in the Mercy King invite you to rethink your own relationship with doubt, fear, or control?
3. What small act of obedience might reflect a surrendered heart, a quiet yes that joins you to the redemptive work of God in the world?

One Action Step

This week name one area of your life where ruthless trust feels especially hard. Write out your honest doubts, fears, or questions, then bring them before God in prayer. Ask the Spirit for courage to take just one step forward in trust. Whether that step looks like confession, repair, letting go, or saying yes to something costly, trust that the Mercy King who met Mary in her uncertainty will meet you in yours—with mercy in one hand and invitation in the other.

MOVEMENT THREE

The Hope That Holds Us

NINE

When You're Tired of Pretending

The Mercy King Who Ends the Performance Game

> All sins are attempts to fill voids. Because we cannot stand the God-shaped hole inside of us, we try stuffing it with all sorts of things, but only God may fill it.
>
> —Simone Weil, *Waiting for God*

Swimming sensation Michael Phelps had it all: global fame, generational talent, and more Olympic gold medals than anyone in history. From the outside looking in, his life was the picture of triumph. He had reached the pinnacle of athletic achievement, admired and celebrated around the world.

And yet not long after his final victory, the silence became deafening.

When the cameras turned off and the cheering faded, Phelps

spiraled into a deep depression. Stripped of the roar of the crowd, he found himself adrift, unsure of who he was apart from his accomplishments. He described the feeling as emptiness—like a man who had gained everything, only to realize he'd lost himself along the way. "I didn't want to be alive," he later confessed in an interview. "I was so lost . . . so helpless."[1]

His self-worth had become so intertwined with performance that once the medals were hung and the accolades quieted, so did his sense of identity. "What now?" he wondered. "Who am I when I'm no longer winning?"

In the depths of his struggle, Phelps began a journey of healing, helped in part by a friend who gave him *The Purpose Driven Life* by Rick Warren, a book that introduced him to the hope and meaning found in Christ. While Phelps hasn't publicly identified as a Christian, that experience helped him realize that his worth was defined not by medals or fame but by a greater purpose beyond himself, one that Christians understand as being found in Jesus.[2]

Most of us will never be Olympic athletes, but we know a similar feeling. The promotion we thought would fulfill us becomes just another rung on an endless ladder. The affirmation we hoped would sustain us vanishes with our next mistake. The accomplishment we believed would secure our worth fades faster than we expected.

We all long to hear it: "You are enough. You *do* have what it takes." But even when the praises arrive, their impact rarely lasts. The satisfaction is fleeting. The applause, like Phelps discovered, eventually stops.

And so we return, again and again, to the courtroom of our own making. It's the courtroom of self-justification, hoping this time we'll be able to make our case stick. This dynamic—this innate need to prove ourselves—is not new.

It was the struggle of sixteenth-century German monk Martin Luther too. For years he wore himself down trying to be good enough for God. But the harder he worked, the more aware he became of how much he fell short. Then, through his study of Paul's letter to the Romans, he experienced a breakthrough: "The righteous will live by faith" (Rom. 1:17).

For Luther, this became a day of liberation. He later wrote, "When I discovered this, I was born again of the Holy Ghost, and the doors of paradise swung open, and I walked through."[3] He went on to champion justification by faith as the doctrine on which the church stands or falls. Still today it's also the doctrine on which *we* stand or fall.

We may affirm grace—God's free gift of justification or righteousness based on faith in Christ alone—with our lips, but our hearts easily drift back to self-justification—trying to prove ourselves, striving to be enough, hoping that our goodness and track record will quiet our guilt, soothe our insecurities, and silence our fear of not measuring up.

What we believe about God—and about ourselves—shows up in all kinds of ways: in the pressure to perform at work, the desire to impress in social settings by saying something insightful or cracking a funny joke, the impulse to curate the perfect image. The verdict always seems just out of reach. No résumé, moral stature, or social validation can silence the fear that whatever the standard is, we don't measure up.

Paul puts it bluntly: "Where, then, is boasting? It is excluded" (Rom. 3:27). In the courtroom of justification by grace through faith, there is no room for pride, only for humble gratitude.

Still we resist. We cling to our self-justifying credentials as proof—to God, to others, and to ourselves—that we are worthy in and of ourselves, based on what *we* bring to the table. In Paul's day believers looked to circumcision and law-keeping. Today we look to whatever a jury of our peers would consider praiseworthy or of note. But the ultimate standard that applies to us all results in a verdict that is equally universal: "All have sinned and fall short of the glory of God" (Rom. 3:23). No matter how hard we try, we cannot put ourselves together—let alone keep ourselves together—to meet the standard set by our Creator, which is the standard of perfection. Unless an outside source steps in and credits us with a record we could never achieve on our own, we are without hope.

Strangely this is good news for us.

If righteousness must be earned, we are in deep trouble. But if righteousness is a gift—freely given by the Mercy King, who lived the perfect life we couldn't and died the death we deserved—then we can finally rest. We can stop performing. Stop pretending. And we can lay down the burden of trying to be enough.

Justification by faith is not God saying, "Try harder." It's God saying, "I see you. I love you. I accept and receive you, not because of what you've done but because of what Jesus, the Mercy King, has done on your behalf."

Our Problem with Boasting

Our struggle for approval is nothing new. Long before performance reviews and internet likes and follows, Paul named the same human tendency: to base our worth on what we do, rather than on what God has done. He called it boasting. And whether it's religious or nonreligious in nature, we all do it. We're all looking for evidence that, as the pathetic *Saturday Night Live* self-help character Stuart Smalley would say while looking in the mirror, "I'm good enough, smart enough, and doggone it, people like me."[4]

In his teaching on justification by faith, Paul highlights two kinds of boasting that we must leave behind. The first is religious boasting, which seeks worth through spiritual accomplishments. The second is existential boasting, which seeks worth through nonreligious achievements and the approval of other people. While these forms may look different on the surface, both originate from the same internal pressure to prove ourselves, to merit acceptance, to validate our existence through our own effort and likability.

Religious Boasting

Let's begin with religious boasting. In Romans 3:29–30, Paul addresses circumcision, a physical sign of the Old Testament covenant with God, akin to baptism in the New Testament. Over time, circumcision came to represent more than Jewish identity; it marked a way of life shaped by rituals, feasts, and laws. For some these external markers became more than covenant signs; they became requirements for belonging. God's acceptance, in their minds, was reserved for those inside the circle of circumcision—which became code for those who had the right background, ethnicity, and nationality, who practiced the right customs, and who followed the right rules.

Paul, once a highly respected rabbi himself, challenges this way of thinking head on: "Is God the God of Jews only? Is he not the God of Gentiles too? Yes, of Gentiles too" (Rom. 3:29–30). This would have landed like a thunderclap to many in his audience. Some rabbis of the time even prayed, "Blessed are you, Lord our God, King of the Universe, who has not made me a Gentile . . . who has not made me a slave . . . who has not made me a woman."[5]

Victor Hugo's *Les Misérables* offers a haunting portrait of this boasting mindset in the character of Inspector Javert. Driven by duty and obsessed with order, Javert builds his life on the belief that respectability is earned by strict justice. We might say he was a proponent of justification by rules-keeping. In his world, mercy is weakness, and criminals like Jean Valjean should be punished, not pardoned.

But when Valjean ascends to a position of authority and shows Javert radical mercy—sparing him when he has every right to crush him—Javert's entire framework collapses. He cannot reconcile a world where forgiveness trumps punishment, compassion outweighs condemnation, and mercy triumphs over judgment. Valjean's merciful gesture unravels him. Internally, he is tormented. Relationally, he is isolated. He cannot accept kindness that is unearned, nor live in a world where such kindness even exists. In the end his inability to receive mercy leaves him broken, in an emotional torture chamber of his own making. Javert's story is a tragic reminder: Self-righteousness may feel like strength, but it usually masks deep insecurity—and it leaves no room for healing and redemption, no room for connection, and no room for God.[6]

This same dynamic can quietly infiltrate the church. Even the most devoted Christians are not immune. We may not boast with our words, but inwardly we keep score—church attendance, charitable giving, theological precision, spiritual discipline, and the big one: not screwing up publicly. It's no surprise, then, that church involvement continues to decline, and one Barna report shows that 42 percent of full-time pastors have seriously considered leaving ministry.[7]

Church attendance, charitable giving, and spiritual discipline are of course good things in and of themselves. But even devotion can become a form of boasting if it becomes the basis of our confidence rather than the fruit of our dependence.

True righteousness, the kind that makes us right with God, calls for a purity of thought, word, and deed that none of us can reach on our own. We need the Mercy King to stand in the gap on our behalf.

Paul drives this home in his letter to the Romans. Religious rituals and spiritual résumés, no matter how impressive, cannot establish our standing before God. Jesus himself *is* the standard, and nothing we do can elevate us to his level. Paul's message is both sobering and freeing: a self-justifying faith built on our morality, our religious effort, or our "good person" vibes will never be enough. The only way forward is to surrender our self-reliance and receive the gift of God's grace through faith in the finished work of the Mercy King.

Existential Boasting

Paul's message in Romans also uncovers a more subtle form of self-justification, what we might call existential boasting. Unlike religious boasting, which relies on perceived spiritual or moral credentials, existential boasting seeks to prove worth through success, image management, productivity, or personal achievement. It's less overtly religious, but every bit as insidious and widespread.

We began this chapter with one example of existential boasting. While Martin Luther's crisis of the soul was rooted in religious striving—trying to earn God's favor through spiritual rigor—Michael Phelps's struggle reflected a different kind of desperation: the relentless need to justify one's existence through achievement, performance, and acclaim.

In Romans 3:25 (ESV) Paul uses the word *propitiation*, which means the removal of wrath. For a first-century audience, especially in Rome, this word would have stirred images of pagan gods—moody, unpredictable deities whose wrath needed to be appeased with endless sacrifice. These gods bore little resemblance to the Mercy King; they were more like emotional tyrants, always demanding more, and never satisfied.

Each of these gods embodied a specific domain of human longing or prowess. Mars, the god of war, promised favor to those who were strong and fearless in battle. Aphrodite, the goddess of love and beauty, required physical allure and romantic conquest. Hermes, the swift-footed messenger god, presided over commerce and communication, favoring cleverness and strategy. Nike, the goddess of victory, bestowed her approval on those at the top of their game, whether they were athletes, warriors, or artists. To stay justified before such gods, you had to be exceptional—and keep proving it. Acceptance was never freely given. It was earned. And always at risk of being taken away.

In such a world there is no room for a God whose defining attribute is mercy.

At first glance ancient paganism may seem foreign to our modern sensibilities. A secular person today might say, "I don't believe in gods who need to be appeased, or that people have to perform to be accepted." But is that entirely true?

Even in a post-religious age, we continue to build our own sacrificial systems—modern rituals through which we seek favor and avoid rejection. The names of our gods have changed, but the demands remain strikingly familiar: "Thou shalt be successful, beautiful, wealthy, important, famous, powerful, hardworking, relevant, physically fit, street savvy, book smart . . ." The list is endless. And the expectations are high.

To stay in their favor, we sacrifice time, rest, relationships—even our own health—in the hope of receiving what these gods falsely promise. Like the ancients, so many of us live with a fear of falling short of something, and of disappointing someone in the process. We work hard to measure up, as if our value depends on our performance.

Whether or not we are religious, the ache for justification runs deep in every human heart.

In a moment of raw honesty, Oprah Winfrey once shared that after nearly every interview—whether it was with a former or sitting president, a famous actor, a beautiful model, a hilarious comedian, a bestselling author, or an award-winning musician—each guest would ask the same question as soon as the cameras stopped rolling: "How was that? Was that okay? How'd I do?"[8]

Beneath all the charisma, acclaim, and accomplishment, even the world's most notable winners crave affirmation. Despite achieving their goals, many remain haunted by an invisible standard that whispers to their hearts, "You are still not enough."

Oprah herself has shared that when she realized her weight had crept past two hundred pounds, her first response was self-directed shame: "I was stressed and I was frustrated and quite frankly I was actually embarrassed."[9] Why? Because she knew the unspoken rules of American show-business culture, a modern version of an ancient false god that says you are worthy only if you meet certain physical expectations. Today's gods don't demand burnt offerings, but they do demand a certain image.

When we fall short of that image, we feel it in our guts and bones—as if we've failed to make the required sacrifice and will certainly be punished for it. Shamed. Belittled. Disregarded. Erased.

This is why so many overwork, overexercise, undereat, and obsess about image. We are driven by an internal voice that says, "If you don't measure up, you'll be finished." It's as if we're still offering sacrifices—not to ancient idols but to the faceless, harsh, judgmental expectations of our age. In pursuit of validation, we surrender our peace, our rest, and even our relationships.

Scripture has a name for this: the "fear of man" (Prov. 29:25), which is the self-defeating, anxiety-inducing belief that our worth is determined by the opinions of others rather than by the voice of God. It's the compulsion to shape our lives around human approval, to let others' verdicts define who we are. We look to our bosses, our peers, or the internet to tell us we matter. But beneath it all, we're asking a single aching question: "Have I done enough to be seen as worthy?"

We like to think of ourselves as free, but in truth, many of us live as captives—enslaved not to literal gods but to public opinion, performance metrics, and internal pressure and shame. It's a form of wrath from false, modern gods. We no longer offer animal sacrifices or cut ourselves with stones, but we do sacrifice time, energy, and wholeness in the desperate hope that our efforts will be enough to secure love, respect, or peace.

And yet, even after all this striving, we still fall short.

Justification by Faith in Christ Alone

What's the answer to the draining cycle of self-justification? Paul points us to a radical alternative: *sola fide*—"faith alone." In Romans 3:25 (ESV) he writes of "propitiation by his blood," referring to Jesus' once-for-all sacrifice on the cross. Unlike the endless offerings demanded by ancient pagan gods—or the unrelenting expectations of modern life, including those we place on ourselves—Christ's self-giving is final and fully sufficient. Through his blood, he has removed the threat of God's wrath for all who trust in him.

What kind of king justifies the guilty at the cost of himself? This is where the Mercy King steps in. He uses his royal power not to crush and imprison but to acquit, redeem, and release. He upholds justice by absorbing its full weight at the cross, and then turns to offer us his perfect record in exchange for our broken one. It was a onetime act with eternal effect. His royal decree over our salvation cannot be undone. No sin, no doubt, no failure can overturn his verdict: "I hereby pronounce you, the defendant . . ."

Forgiven. Righteous. Beloved.

The Mercy King does not merely extend grace, he enthrones it, ensuring that no accusation can stand against those he has justified.

When Jesus cried out from the cross, "My God, my God, why have you forsaken me?" (Mark 15:34), he bore the full weight of judgment on our behalf. That anguished cry holds the key to our peace: He endured the separation we deserved so that we would never have to. As Isaiah foretold, "the punishment that brought us peace was on him" (Isa. 53:5). The condemnation meant for us fell on him. In its place we are given rest.

And what is our part in receiving this gift of justification? It's surprisingly simple: We bring nothing. No effort. No accolades. No résumés. No self-validating credentials. Just empty, open hands and receptive hearts. We come not as achievers but as sons and daughters, "little children"—needy, dependent, and unafraid to admit it. As the old hymn confesses, "Nothing in my hands I bring; simply to the cross I cling."

Whether through religious striving or worldly success, every path of self-justification leads to the same weary destination. Each demands that we earn a worthiness only God can give, the worthiness that says, "In Christ you are enough. In Christ you are loved. In Christ you are accepted and received." Justification by faith invites us to release our exhausting strategies and rest in the verdict he has already secured.

We no longer need to strive for God's love or chase the approval of others. We are free to live from a place of secure acceptance.

A Verdict We Must Receive

The courtroom is closed. The judge has spoken. The case is settled. And the verdict is in. You are declared, through Jesus, forgiven, righteous, and beloved. Not by your own doing but by the King's decree. No more striving. No more proving. Only resting in the mercy of the King.

This verdict is anchored entirely in Jesus Christ—his flawless life lived on our behalf and his sacrificial death endured for us. Through faith we receive propitiation, the removal of sin's penalty. But this gift is more than mere forgiveness. It's forgiveness plus. Our guilt is not only erased, it's replaced with a positive standing before God (2 Cor. 5:21). We are given a righteousness that comes from outside ourselves. Martin Luther called it an "alien righteousness"—a validating performance record not earned by us but given to us by the Mercy King. This righteousness defines us, qualifies us, and gives us permanent access to God, not because of our merit but because of his mercy.

But how can we grasp such an undeserved gift?

A picture might help.

Each fall, as the temperatures dropped, I used to pull out my bright orange Princeton sweatshirt, given to me by a group of Princeton students after a speaking engagement on their campus. I'd wear it around town—running errands, seeing friends, going to the gym. My wife, Patti, loved to tease me about it, gently reminding me of something I already knew: I didn't go to Princeton. Her playful ribbing always carried a wink of truth: By wearing the sweatshirt, I was implying credentials that I didn't have. A kind of academic version of what military personnel call stolen valor. I'm not, nor have I ever been, an Ivy League student or scholar.

And yet the righteousness of Christ functions just like that—but without the pretense. It's a kind of divinely conferred valor. Not something we earn but something freely given.

A few years ago Patti and I attended Yom Kippur services with a Jewish friend. It was a moving glimpse of God's grace woven into the ancient Day of Atonement rituals. Central to the observance is the act of transferring the people's sins onto a scapegoat, which is then led away, symbolically carrying the community's guilt. Once each year, the people were granted a clean slate. It's a vivid foreshadowing of the gospel. Only in Christ, it's not once a year. It's once and for all. He not only removes our sin but also clothes us in a righteousness we didn't earn.

The gospel, in essence, is a divine exchange of attire. As Paul writes, "God made him who had no sin to be sin for us, so that in him we might become the righteousness of God" (2 Cor. 5:21). We come to God clothed in the rags of our guilt, shame, and regret. Christ steps in, removes those garments, and takes them upon himself. In return he robes us in his own perfection, a spotless covering that gives us a new identity and a validation we could never achieve on our own.

Feeling inadequate? Jesus covers you.

Burdened by shame or failure? He credits you with his perfect record.

Like my Princeton sweatshirt, the righteousness of Christ isn't earned. But unlike my sweatshirt, it's no pretense. It's more like an honorary degree, a doctorate Jesus earned in our name. Through him we are given the standing of a valedictorian, MVP, or medal winner—not in the eyes of man but in the eyes of God, and of the great cloud of witnesses who have gone before us in the journey of grace.

This "validating performance record"[10] of Jesus doesn't merely forgive, it elevates. It makes us not just accepted but cherished. Not just pardoned but delighted in.

Titus 3:5 captures it succinctly: "He saved us, not because of righteous things we had done, but because of his mercy." Jesus' mercy leaves no room for boasting. Paul, writing to a status-driven Roman audience, asks, "What becomes of our boasting?" and answers plainly, "It is excluded" (Rom. 3:27 ESV). Why? Because none of us has what it takes to bridge the gap between ourselves and God on our own.

Imagine two people trying to leap across the Grand Canyon. A small child might clear a few inches; an Olympic long jumper might soar twenty-nine feet. But both still fall fatally short. So it is with us: "All have sinned and fall short of the glory of God." No matter how good we think we are, being good will never be good enough.

Some may appear to stand on higher moral ground than others, but in the end the distance between us and God is too great for any of us to cross on our own. What we need is not more effort but more honesty. Not a better performance but a surrendered heart. We must come as we are, bringing our need, not our résumés, as our offering.

As an old hymn reminds us:

> Not the labor of my hands
> Can fulfill thy law's demands.

Our hope is not in what we do but in what Christ has done—for us, instead of us, and once for all.

A Faith That Is Enough

The gospel isn't about relentless striving—like the "little engine that could," always pushing forward, chanting, "I think I can." Faith in the Mercy King moves in the opposite direction. It begins with admitting our limits. It's more like the "little engine that couldn't"—who finally discovered the deeper truth: We can't, but God can. This pressure-releasing reality—that weak, imperfect, mustard seed–sized faith is still enough (Matt. 17:20)—appears again and again in Jesus' encounters throughout the Gospels.

Take the desperate father in Mark 9:14–29, who brings his tormented son to Jesus. After watching the disciples fail to heal him, his faith is hanging by a thread. "If you can do anything, have compassion on us and help us," he pleads (v. 22 ESV). Jesus replies, "'If you can!' All things are possible for one who believes." And then comes one of the most honest confessions in all of Scripture: "I believe; help my unbelief!" Jesus responds not with rebuke but with mercy, and heals the boy. The father's faith wasn't strong at all, only strong enough to cry out for mercy. And it was more than sufficient.

Or consider the Canaanite woman in Matthew 15:21–28, a mother fighting for her daughter's life. At first Jesus seems to dismiss her, but she presses on, insisting that even a crumb of his mercy would be sufficient. Her persistence isn't pride, it's desperation rooted in trust. She knows she has nothing to offer and everything to receive. Jesus praises her faith and grants her request.

Then there's Peter, sinking in the waves. He has the courage to step out of the boat but quickly panics when the wind rises. "Lord, save me!" he cries as he begins to go under. Instantly Jesus reaches out his hand. Peter's faith wavers, but it is directed toward the right object—and that is all that is needed to save him.

Even frail, faltering faith is enough when it rests in the right object. What matters most is not the strength of our faith but the strength of the one in whom we place it. It is not our grip on Christ that saves us but his grip on us. The trembling father who cried, "I believe; help my unbelief!" received the mercy of healing in that very moment not because he believed perfectly but because he turned his cry in the direction of the Mercy King.

A friend once shared with me a letter from a father to his son, who was struggling with depression and doubt. These words captured the effect that justification by grace through faith in Christ alone can have on the human heart:

> In the struggles you face, dear son, I don't want you to ever forget that Moses stuttered, David's armor didn't fit, John Mark was rejected by Paul, Hosea's wife was a prostitute, Amos's only training for prophecy was as a fig tree pruner. Jeremiah struggled with depression, Gideon and Thomas doubted, Jonah ran from God, and Abraham failed miserably in lying, as did his son and grandson. These were real people with real failures and inadequacies, and God shook the earth through them. It is not so much from our strength that he draws but from his invincible might. I am praying that he will give you courage in his strength.

God doesn't demand polished strength. He has always done his best, most defining work through our human weaknesses. As Hemingway put it in *A Farewell to Arms*, "The world breaks everyone, and afterward, many are strong at the broken places."[11] God doesn't require flawless instruments. He works through and on behalf of the flawed ones like us.

The Transforming Power of Grace

This assurance of God's acceptance is not a license to live however we please. Paul anticipates that very objection in Romans: "Do we then overthrow the law by this faith?" Should we ignore God's commands because we're justified by faith alone? His answer is emphatic: "By no means!" (Rom. 3:31 ESV). Knowing we are fully loved and accepted by God is no reason for apathy. Rather it awakens a desire to live in harmony with the one who loves us and gave himself completely for us.

As Martin Luther is often quoted as saying, "We are saved by faith alone, but not by a faith that is alone." Real faith doesn't just justify us, it changes us, first at the level of our affections and then, over time, in our thoughts, words, and actions. As pastor and Bible teacher James Montgomery Boice once wrote, "The truly born-again person now pursues intensely what he or she previously despised."[12] Once our lives are in the hands of the Mercy King, the sins that once enticed us lose their grip, while virtues we once ignored draw us in. Full transformation doesn't happen overnight; but over time, faith in Jesus reshapes the heart.

And if the mercy that transforms hasn't melted and changed your heart yet, know this: Jesus still invites you to come to him with your own version of the prayer "Lord, I believe; help my unbelief." As you take this simple step, he pledges to clothe you in his righteousness—a spotless wedding garment, symbolizing your new identity in him.

Fleming Rutledge puts it like this: "The essence of what it means to be a Christian is that we do not stand on our own. We do not present our credentials to God. We do not bring anything in our hands. Instead, we appear before the judgment seat under the banner of the cross, pleading nothing but what Jesus Christ has done for us."[13]

Once we've been washed by mercy and grace, we no longer live defined by shame or guilt, and our hearts can be un-heavied by it. The record of our failures is rewritten: perfect and complete, based on the finished work of Christ. We can stand before God unashamed with hearts uplifted and heads held high because our new identity and secure future is fixed.

The weight is lifted. The striving can stop. The courtroom is empty now—no judge, no jury, no more evidence against you. The gavel has fallen, once and for all. Under the reign of Jesus, the Mercy King, the law has no jurisdiction, demands to measure up have no claim, and joy is within reach.

But the question remains: Will you let yourself live as though the case is closed?

Will you step out of the courtroom of self-justification and into the freedom that the Mercy King has secured for you? Will you show up—at church, at work, and in the various arenas of life—as one who is forgiven, righteous, and beloved in his eyes? It is for freedom that Christ has set you free. From today forward, may you live in that freedom and resist every impulse to return to the courtroom.

Summary

We live in a world that constantly tells us to prove ourselves—through success, performance, appearance, and even spiritual devotion. But the gospel of Jesus Christ offers us a better word: justification by faith alone. In the eyes of the Mercy King, we are declared righteous not because of what we've done but because of what Christ has done for us. His verdict—forgiven, righteous, beloved—is final and cannot be reversed. Whether our boasting is religious or existential, it will always leave us empty. But faith in Christ frees us from the courtroom of self-justification and places us securely in the grace of the King, who took our judgment and gave us his own righteousness. In him even weak and faltering faith is enough. In him we are invited to rest.

Three Questions

1. Where do you most feel the pressure to prove yourself? Is it in your job, your parenting, your appearance, your moral performance, or something else? How is that pressure affecting your heart?
2. What difference does it make to know that your righteousness is a gift, not a goal? How might your spiritual life, relationships, and sense of identity change if you truly lived from this truth?
3. How do you respond to the idea that even imperfect faith—faith mixed with doubt, weakness, or fear—is enough when it's placed in Jesus? What does this reveal about the character of Christ and about the nature of real faith?

One Action Step

This week name one area in your life where you feel pressure to perform or measure up. Write it down. Then, in a quiet moment of prayer, surrender that area to Jesus. Say to him, "Lord, here is where I've been trying to prove myself. I give it to you. Cover me with your mercy and remind me that your righteousness is enough."

Afterward share this act of surrender with a trusted friend, mentor, or small group member who can walk with you and remind you that the courtroom is closed—and the verdict is in.

TEN

When You Have Nothing Left to Give

The Mercy King Who Reignites Dead Hearts

> We delight in the beauty of the butterfly, but rarely admit the changes it has gone through to achieve that beauty. Life's challenges and pains shape us, but God's grace is the cocoon where true beauty, resilience, and love come to life. We are all works in progress, masterpieces not yet complete.
>
> —Maya Angelou, *Letter to My Daughter*

Let's start with a scene from *Dumb and Dumber*, because strangely enough it fits.

It's a moment that captures the essence of unrealistic hope. In the film, Jim Carrey's character, Lloyd Christmas, is hopelessly infatuated with a woman named Mary Swanson. Clinging to the fantasy that they might end up together, he asks her, "What do you think the chances are of a guy like you and a girl like me ending up together?" Trying to be kind, Mary replies, "Not good." Lloyd presses, "You mean, not good like one in a hundred?" She clarifies, "I'd say more like one in a million." His face lights up. "So you're telling me there's a chance! Yeah!"[1]

We've all known that kind of blind hope, whether as the one holding on or the one who gently lets someone down. But now imagine the reverse: not slim odds but none. Picture someone who is incapacitated, with no possibility of healing or recovery. According to Scripture this is our natural condition before God—not just uninterested, not merely resistant, but spiritually dead. Lifeless in our sins. Incapable of seeking him, serving him, or loving him, no matter how deep his affection for us.

This condition—often called "human depravity" or "spiritual inability"—means that our chances of choosing God on our own aren't one in a million. They're zero. As Jesus says in John 6:44, "No one can come to me unless the Father who sent me draws them." The word *can* here speaks not of permission but of ability. Left to ourselves, we simply lack the capacity. Our separation from God isn't a matter of mood or preference, it's a matter of impairment.

Without divine intervention, our hearts drift toward anything but God. As Paul tells us in Romans, we suppress the truth about him and exchange it for lies, turning our worship toward the creation and away from the Creator (Rom. 1:25). It's why we chase approval that never satisfies, distract ourselves endlessly, or cling to control even as it wears us out. We don't merely forget God, we resist him, until he awakens something new in us.

And awaken us, he does.

In that same passage from John 6, Jesus adds a promise: "All those the Father gives me *will* come to me" (v. 37, emphasis added). Those whom God calls will respond. If you are a follower of Christ, there came a time when your heart shifted from apathy to desire, from resistance to longing. That shift wasn't self-generated. It wasn't your willpower. It was his mercy and grace. God drew you to himself. You moved from no chance to certainty. From spiritual death to life. Why? Because he loved you first. "We love because he first loved us" (1 John 4:19).

Here we will explore what happens when his kind pursuit meets our dead passivity, when the Mercy King calls to the spiritually unresponsive and breathes life where there was none. This is no sentimental kindness. It's resurrection power wrapped in royal mercy.

Traditionally this idea is called irresistible grace, though "effectual calling" may better capture its meaning. The term *irresistible* can be misunderstood, as though people never resist God. They do. *We* do. But effectual calling speaks to the outcome. When God sets his heart on us, his pursuit is always effective. He never fails to reach the ones he calls. As Bonhoeffer once wrote, "The call of Christ transforms everything: our hearts, our hopes, and even our resistance. It isn't that we can't resist God's love; rather, it's that his love becomes irresistible, melting our defenses and calling us to a life far beyond what we could have imagined for ourselves."[2]

If God has set his heart on drawing you, he will. Gently, yet with determined resolve. He does not merely extend a hand, he issues a summons. He is both the Lover who woos us and the King who conquers us. His mercy is not soft or uncertain. It is sovereign. And when he calls, it is not a suggestion. It is a King's invitation that reclaims what is already his.

This love does not coerce. It captivates.

And when it does, the effect is that we obey his summons, "Come to me."

By our fallen nature, we live under a kind of spell—a resistance to grace, a pull toward self-rule, an allergic aversion to God's holiness. Like prodigals our hearts push back against his care and character and wander far from home. But when God sets his affection on us and opens our hearts to receive it, the spell is broken. His grace doesn't barge in, it gently overcomes. It doesn't erase our will, it awakens our desire. What once felt irrelevant now becomes necessary. What we once resisted, we now crave.

In this way the gift of mercy is a miracle.

The King who commands also woos.

The one who reigns also redeems.

Dead on Arrival: Why We Need a Mercy King

We are not spiritually sick. We are spiritually dead.

But the Mercy King doesn't leave us there. Into our lifelessness, God speaks. Into our cold resistance, he warmly breathes. Into our downward spiral comes a divine interruption. Two simple words—*but God*—break open the tombs of our lives and let resurrection light pour in. These words are more than theology. They are the hinge on which every Christian story turns. *But God*, the Mercy King, comes to resurrect.

He doesn't just make bad people better, he makes dead people alive.

This is why we mustn't treat the gospel like a self-help manual or a directive to try harder. The Mercy King doesn't show up with a checklist for us to measure up to. He shows up with breath for dry bones, with life where there was no pulse (Ezek. 37:1–14).

Left to ourselves—even when we are at our most disciplined and sincere—we resist him. Jesus said it clearly: "Apart from me you can do nothing" (John 15:5). The apostle Paul knew this firsthand. Once a zealous rabbi, convinced he was alive to God, Paul later looked back and described those years as a kind of living death and himself as a dead man walking.

Paul gives voice to his and our human plight in Ephesians 2: "As for you, you were dead in your transgressions and sins, in which you used to live when you followed the ways of this world. . . . All of us also lived among them at one time, gratifying the cravings of our flesh and following its desires and thoughts" (Eph. 2:1–3).

This isn't a temporary slump or a string of poor decisions. Paul is describing a settled state—spiritual stillbirth, lifelessness—that only God can interrupt. And into that death, God steps in to insert himself, not with condemnation but with mercy. Not with demands but with deliverance. Not with finger-pointing but with nail-scarred hands. *But God.*

Late Anglican pastor and theologian John Stott captured this reality with piercing clarity. Reflecting on Ephesians 2, he wrote, "We need to be clear that this is a description of everybody. It's a description of the universal human condition." He paints the picture this way:

> One person may have the vigorous body of an athlete, another the lively mind of a scholar, and a third the vivacious personality of a film star. Are we to say that such people, if Christ has not saved them, are dead? Yes, indeed, we must and do say this very thing. They have no life. They are blind to the glory of Jesus Christ, deaf to the voice of the Holy Spirit, with no love for God, no sensitive awareness of his personal reality, no leaping of their spirit toward him, and no longing for fellowship with him and his people. They are as unresponsive to him as a corpse. It is a living death, and those who live it are dead even while they are still living.[3]

Words like these are jarring in their bluntness and grimness, especially in a culture that prizes health, achievement, and moral respectability as signs of vitality. But as I once heard in a sermon, there are degrees of sickness, but dead is dead. A person with terminal cancer is gravely ill; someone with a cold is only mildly unwell. But a well-dressed, made-up corpse is just as dead as a murder victim in a backstreet alley.

Sickness may vary, but death is absolute.

Scripture teaches that even our good deeds can carry the scent of death. We may try to appear whole on the outside, but beneath the surface, something essential is missing. You can repaint the walls, light a candle, and open the windows to let the sun in, but if the foundation is crumbling or there is mold inside the framing, the house still isn't safe to live in. In the same way, we can polish up our behavior, flatter with our words, and pursue a well-behaved life, but without the renewing presence of Christ, our hearts remain untouched. It's not bad people who need improvement, it's dead people who need resurrection. And only the Mercy King is capable of pulling it off.

Apart from Christ we are not just misguided or slightly off course, we are dead in our transgressions and sins (Eph. 2:1). No amount of self-help, coaching, therapy, or even Bible study can fix this. Like a corpse, we are helpless to revive ourselves. We don't just need a little push in the right direction, we need a miracle. The Mercy King must ignite our hearts with his truth, beauty, and love. Without him we remain unable even to want him.

But the good news is this: It is when we are most powerless that the Mercy King steps in. He does for us what we cannot do for ourselves, and he does within us what we cannot stir up within ourselves. Because of him, what was once dead in us now lives.

The Royal Intervention

The words *but God* signal more than a rescue; they also announce a re-creation. The same mercy that pulls us out of the grave also reshapes us from the inside out. We are not only made alive but raised, seated with Christ, and identified as his workmanship, his masterpiece. His living poetry (Eph. 2:10).

The Mercy King doesn't merely interrupt our deaths, he initiates a brand-new life.

Paul writes, "If anyone is in Christ, he is a new creation; the old has passed away; behold, the new has come" (2 Cor. 5:17 ESV). God doesn't just forgive our past, he reshapes our present and secures our future. He works intimately within us to change what we love, what we value, and how we live. What once seemed irrelevant or even unattractive to us—God's holiness, his nearness, his voice—becomes lovely and desirable. What once drew us in now starts to lose its grip.

Pastor James Montgomery Boice once described this as the moment when "boring grace becomes amazing grace."[4] Grace, once a doctrine to understand, now becomes a delight to experience. The sins that once enticed us begin to look absurd. We start to see them as they really are: empty, destructive, unworthy of our energy and affection.

This was Martin Luther's experience too. As we explored earlier, he lived under the weight of guilt and fear, unable to find peace no matter how many confessions of sin he offered. When asked if he loved God, his reply was heartbreakingly candid: "Love God? I hate him." But as he studied Paul's letter to the Romans, something shifted. The law that had once condemned him gave way to grace that freed him. Reflecting on his experience, Luther wrote, "Thereupon I felt myself to be reborn, and to have gone through open doors into paradise. The whole of Scripture took on a new meaning, and whereas before the justice of God had filled me with hate, now it became to me inexpressibly sweet in greater love."[5]

The gospel had not changed. Luther had. Grace touched his heart in ways that striving never could. This is how grace behaves. It doesn't stand at a distance, waiting for us to get it right. It runs to meet us, wraps us in mercy, and rewrites our stories. Paul describes it simply: "It is by grace you have been saved, through faith—and this is not from yourselves, it is the gift of God—not by works, so that no one can boast" (Eph. 2:8–9). God's love is not something we achieve. It is something we receive.

The real question isn't, "What have I done to deserve this?" but rather, "Why does God love me?" And the answer—both humbling and moving—is this: God loves you not because of anything you've done but simply because he has chosen to love you.

It's a mystery you'll never fully grasp, but it's true.

If you've ever wondered whether you've gone too far, become too broken, or grown too indifferent to the things of God, know this: You haven't. He loved you at your lowest. He loved you at your deadest. And he loves you right now.

Paul restates this in Titus 3:5, the verse anchoring this entire book: "He saved us, not because of righteous things we had done, but because of his mercy." God's love doesn't flow from our goodness, it flows from his. While we were still lifeless in sin, he stepped in—not because we were lovely but because he *is* love (1 John 4:8).

The film *Wonder* offers a tender glimpse of this kind of mercy and love. It tells the story of Auggie Pullman, a young boy born with a severe facial disfigurement. After years of being homeschooled and shielded from the judgment of others, Auggie prepares to enter a traditional school for the first time as a fifth grader. His parents try to cheer him on, but Auggie knows what's coming. And sure enough, the hallways become a gauntlet of stares, whispers, and outright cruelty. Kids avoid sitting next to him. Some laugh. Others look away in discomfort.

One day the pain becomes too much. He comes home in tears and collapses into his mother's arms, saying, "I don't ever want to go back there again. I'm hideous. I'm ugly. Everyone knows it. I'm a freak."

His mom gently kneels down, looks Auggie in the eye, and says, "You are not ugly." When he replies, "You have to say that because you're my mom," she counters with one of the most moving lines in the film: "It's *because* I'm your mom that I can say these things. I know you better than anyone else."

That moment becomes a turning point not just in Auggie's story but in the stories of those around him. Over time the same classmates who once ridiculed him see him differently. They change not because Auggie becomes someone new but because they finally see who he truly is. Courageous. Kind. Honest. Funny. A kid worth knowing. A friend worth having. And in the end, a mirror reflecting the parts of themselves they'd rather not face.

The film ends with a line that tells the truth about us all: "Everyone, even the bullies, is fighting a hard, hidden battle."[6]

Jesus, the Mercy King, understands the battles we fight, even the ones we hide. He sees behind the masks and into the wounds. And he steps toward us and reminds us that in his eyes, we are forgiven, righteous, and beloved. And? It's *because* we are his children that he can say these things; he knows us better than anyone else.

He brings beauty from our ashes.

Glory from our dust.

A fragrance of grace when we feel ugly.

He doesn't love us in spite of knowing everything about us. He loves us because he does.

When Jesus Looks at Us

When Jesus looks at us, he sees everything—the hurts we carry, the walls we've built, and even the self-contempt that whispers, "You're beyond hope, ugly, unlovable." And yet he does not flinch. He does not pull away. The same King who brings dead hearts to life also calls the doubter to trust, the ashamed to rest, and the fearful to take his hand.

We are God's *poiema*—his workmanship, his masterpiece. The word *poiema* gives us "poem," suggesting artistry, intentionality, and beauty. Jesus sees and knows us not only as we are but as we are becoming: his radiant bride in the making, without spot or blemish, lovely in his sight.

Mercy holds back the judgment we deserve; grace offers blessing we could never earn. Mercy doesn't ignore our flaws. It looks through them with tenderness, recognizing the image of God still imprinted on us. And grace reshapes what is broken. In Christ's hands even our scars become trophies of redemption. God knows us completely and loves us fully. And because he does, he will not leave us where we are. He is making all things, including us, new—gently, gradually, patiently, faithfully.

Like Auggie's mother in *Wonder*, who insists on her son's beauty not in spite of knowing him but because she knows him best, so Jesus looks at us in our frailty and says, "I know you, and I love you." We may protest, pointing to our flaws, our failures, our fears. But he cuts through our self-condemnation with stubborn grace and a redeemed identity.

To the greedy, he says, "You are now generous."

To the impure: "You are now cleansed and radiant."

To the embittered: "You are now a peacemaker."

To the fearful: "You are now brave."

He says these things not because we've arrived but because his love is making them true, slowly but surely and through the passage of time. The Mercy King delights in who we are becoming, even as he embraces us as we are now. As Paul writes, "He who began a good work in you will carry it on to completion" (Phil. 1:6).

We gladly participate in this heart-and-life renewing, renovating work because we've been well loved by the one who was disfigured for us. Jesus, the Man of Sorrows, bore our wounds and carried our shame. The world saw nothing in him to desire, and yet he gave himself fully for us. Now, on the other side of his disfigurement, bullying, and humiliation, we see him differently. The Suffering Servant who once seemed unremarkable is now our deepest joy (Isaiah 53).

The world may look at us and ask, "Why give up so much for him?" And with grace-born clarity, we respond, "Because you don't know him like I do. But would you like to?"

The poet John Donne once wrote, "Except you enthrall me, never shall I be free."[7] That's the potential impact of the gospel upon us: not just that we believe in grace but that we be captivated and changed by it. The Mercy King sees every part of you—every scar, every defense, every impulse to run. And still he moves toward you. Not later. Not when you're better. Now. He's not waiting for a more polished version of you. He wants you as you are.

Will you let him in?

Will you stop resisting and receive the love that has been pursuing you?

May the Mercy King awaken in you a love so real, so compelling, that it turns the ordinary into wonder. May grace cease to feel routine and instead become the song of your soul. And may your life, made alive in Christ, become a living poem, composed by the one who knows you fully, loves you deeply, and is making you whole.

Summary

We don't come to God because we're wise, willing, or spiritually curious. According to Scripture, we are born not merely distant from God but dead—unable to love, trust, or even want him. But God, being rich in mercy, steps in. He awakens our hearts not because we are lovely but because he is love. His grace doesn't merely patch us up, it makes us new. He doesn't just forgive the guilty, he resurrects the dead. In Christ we are not only redeemed, we are recreated. Once spiritually unresponsive, we are now God's living poetry, crafted in grace and called into a life that reflects the heart of the Mercy King. This isn't behavior modification. It's a miracle. It's not self-help. It's resurrection.

Three Questions

1. How does the idea of being spiritually dead, rather than just morally flawed or distant, shift the way you understand your need for God?
2. Have you experienced a moment when God's grace moved from being a concept to something personal, beautiful, and life changing? What did that shift look and feel like?
3. In what areas of your life is God reshaping you from the inside out? What new identity is he speaking over you, even as he loves you as you are?

One Action Step

Choose one lie you've been believing about yourself—something shame filled, fearful, or limiting—and replace it with the truth God declares over you in Christ. Write it down. Speak it aloud.

Then take one small step to live as if it were true. Let your day—your posture, your tone, your decisions—be shaped not by fear or striving but by the voice of the Mercy King, who knows you fully and loves you still.

ELEVEN

When You're Stuck in Stockholm

The Mercy King Who Turns Religion into a Love Affair

> Christ says, "Give me all. I don't want so much of your time and so much of your money and so much of your work: I want you. I have not come to torment your natural self, but to kill it. No half measures are any good."
>
> —C. S. Lewis, *Mere Christianity*

In his letter to the Galatians, Paul confronts a congregation caught in a deep spiritual malaise, what we might call a kind of Stockholm syndrome of the soul.

The term *Stockholm syndrome*, coined after a 1973 bank robbery in Stockholm, Sweden, describes the strange psychological phenomenon in which hostages form emotional bonds—even loyalty—toward their captors. In the original case, the victims refused to testify against the criminals who had deprived them of freedom. Inexplicably, they'd grown attached to the very ones who'd kept them in bondage. Stockholm syndrome reveals a tragic truth about us: We sometimes cling to the familiar confines of captivity rather than risk the uncertainties of freedom.

You may have seen something like this in a more personal context. Picture a woman trapped in a toxic relationship with an abusive boyfriend. She is trapped not with chains or locks but with shame and fear. Her friends see how she's diminished, how the light has gone out in her eyes. They beg her to leave, to break free. But she stays. "He didn't mean it," she says. "He's trying." She's not lying, she's just afraid. Afraid of starting over. Afraid of what life might be without the structure, however painful, that she's come to know. There's something tragically human about preferring familiar pain to unknown healing. We stay in the cage because, over time, the cage feels like home.

Paul sees the Galatian church caught in just such a dynamic, spiritually speaking. Like hostages, they were clinging to beliefs and practices that restricted rather than freed them, choosing tired, rules-bound religion over the liberating grace of Christ.

Their captors were the so-called circumcision party—a group insisting that adherence to certain Mosaic laws, especially circumcision, was necessary for full acceptance into the Christian community. Paul's response is direct and urgent: You are surrendering your freedom. You are trading the life-giving, freedom-advancing rule of the real and present Mercy King, who welcomes the unworthy, for a false law-master who rules by shame, pressure, and exclusion.

As we trace Paul's words through this fiery letter, we see that Jesus, our Mercy King, does not confront the Galatians' bondage with guilt or coercion. He breaks chains with grace. He replaces fear with the promise of family. From his throne he empowers fragile faith and invites those stuck in spiritual captivity to come home.

Paul opens his letter with no pleasantries but with shock and grief. "I am astonished," he writes, "that you are so quickly deserting the one who called you to live in the grace of Christ and are turning to a different gospel" (Gal. 1:6). This is no casual correction or theological footnote. It's a full-on intervention. Paul isn't addressing minor doctrinal disagreements; he's confronting a crisis that threatens the very heart of the gospel and the salvation of those being deceived.

His frustration with the false teachers reaches a boiling point when he says he wishes they would "emasculate themselves" (Gal. 5:12). These are not harmless traditionalists; they are spiritual slavedrivers posing as guides, unauthorized jailers reinforcing chains Jesus came to break. Paul's words are jarring, but they reflect the sobering truth: Bad theology can masquerade as good news and destroy lives in the process. His goal is not only to silence these teachers but to halt the spread of their soul-crushing message altogether.

To suggest that salvation requires anything beyond the finished work of Jesus Christ is a serious distortion. Paul leaves no room for ambiguity: Even if he himself, or "an angel from heaven," were to preach a different message, it must be rejected outright (Gal. 1:6–12). The gospel is beautifully clear: Christ alone saves. Any message that adds to his finished work is a step back into captivity.

To help the Galatians understand the weight of this error, Paul uses the image of a guardian—a stern overseer, rigid and unrelenting. Influenced by the circumcision party, the Galatians had begun to see the law in this way, as something that demanded perfection rather than pointing to grace. They had slipped into a mindset where rules replaced relationship and fear took the place of freedom (Gal. 3:24–29).

But the gospel changes everything. It opens the door to a life marked by grace and release.

Now imagine a prisoner stepping into the sunlight after years behind bars. The gate has swung wide open. Freedom has been declared. And yet he lingers at the threshold, unsure of who he is without the structure of the cell. Though the door is open, he's tempted to return to the life he knows. This is the quiet tragedy of legalism: It can make captivity feel more familiar than the freedom Jesus offers.

Paul longs for the Galatians—and for us—to keep walking forward.

There is someone far greater than the law's demands. He is the Mercy King, who not only unlocks the cell but also prepares a home. He brings more than a pardon, he brings a new identity. In his kingdom we are welcomed as family, robed in righteousness, seated at the table, and given a name that cannot be taken away. The Mercy King lifts the prisoner and places a crown on their head. He welcomes the weary into joy and dignity.

Paul writes with assurance, "Now that faith has come, we are no longer under a guardian" (Gal. 3:25 ESV). The law has served its purpose: to reveal our need and lead us to the one who meets it completely. Now what remains is to walk in the freedom Christ has secured.

In the next several pages we'll explore three dynamics with a view to promote living in freedom: the failure to launch, the failure to thrive, and the way out of spiritual Stockholm syndrome. Paul's message, both then and now, is a call to step fully into the new life offered by Jesus: grounded in grace, sustained by love, and filled with the joy of belonging under the reign of the Mercy King.

Don't settle for anything less.

Failure to Launch

Before we can walk in the freedom Jesus provides, we have to name the subtle forms of captivity that we still cling to. To help the Galatians—and us—understand how deeply the slave mindset can trap the soul, Paul rewinds the story. He knows the rules-bound path intimately because he's walked it. And he knows what it takes to get out.

God's law was given to Israel as a gift, not a burden. The Ten Commandments—recorded in Exodus 20 and Deuteronomy 5—formed a foundation for flourishing. The first four commandments speak to our relationship with God: Worship him alone, reject idols, honor his name, and observe the Sabbath. The remaining six guide our relationships with others: Honor your parents, and do not murder, commit adultery, steal, lie, or covet. These commands, simple and direct, were meant to show us how to live in love.

Later Jesus summarized them with clarity and grace: Love God with your whole being and love your neighbor as yourself. Everything else, he said, flows from that. This is the heart of the law as interpreted by the Mercy King: not a burdensome checklist but a vision for freedom and wholeness. At its best and according to its intent, the law was to lead us into joyful relationships, not weigh us down.

But the religious leaders of Jesus' day had lost the plot. Instead of pointing people to love, they expanded the law into 613 detailed rules, many of which added complexity without clarity. Rather than lifting burdens, they added to them—layer upon layer of regulation that left people exhausted and spiritually paralyzed.

This isn't just a first-century problem. The impulse to turn devotion into obligation spans across eras and generations. In Genesis when the serpent tempts Eve, he distorts God's command and Eve joins in. God had said not to eat from the tree, but Eve adds a detail: "We must not touch it." That wasn't part of the instruction. It came from fear, or maybe control—a subtle attempt to build extra security around obedience. And with that, the seed of legalism was planted. The pattern continued across centuries. By the time of the rabbis, rules multiplied in ways that bordered on the absurd. One Sabbath regulation forbade spitting not out of manners but out of fear that the saliva might fall on soil and accidentally germinate a seed. The fixation on minor external behaviors created an atmosphere where righteousness was measured not by love or transformation but by technical compliance.

This mindset—so prevalent among the parties with sway among the Galatians—equated maturity with meticulous rules-following. It left little space for grace, inner renewal, or relational connection with God or others. Holiness became performative. And in that kind of system, the soul shrivels and suffocates.

Consider Jay Gatsby from *The Great Gatsby*, a man who reinvents himself, amasses wealth, and throws extravagant parties, all in the hope of winning approval, love, and belonging. Every detail of his carefully curated life—his mansion, his clothes, his smile—is part of a grand effort to prove that he's worthy of being chosen. In Gatsby's mind, success is a kind of salvation. If he can just impress enough, achieve enough, shine brightly enough, then perhaps Daisy, the woman he loves, will see him, accept him, and want him.

But despite all he achieves, Gatsby remains on the outside. He's admired by many, known by few, and loved by almost no one. His efforts fall short. The ache of his loneliness persists.[1]

Like many of us, Gatsby is running but never arriving. His résumé is full, but his heart is tired. His story taps into the quiet desperation so many of us carry: the belief that if we just try harder, perform better, or appear more put together, then we'll finally break through. But Scripture tells a different story. It repeatedly warns us about the futility of trying to earn love or acceptance through performance. It reminds us that real belonging cannot be bought or achieved. It must be received—freely, by grace.

The Mercy King trades not in merit but in kindness and

hospitality. And for those who come to him weary from striving, he offers something far better than validation. He offers welcome.

The Galatians had fallen into a Gatsby-like, exhausting pursuit. Faith, for them, had become a ladder to climb rather than a bed to rest in. Like Gatsby they were working hard but missing the point. The law had become a means of earning love rather than a path to knowing God. And in doing so, they had lost the joy and ease of grace. Their checklist approach to faith left them stuck, bound by a system that could never give what their hearts most needed.

More Than We Can Bear

The law with all its demands is more than we can carry. It was never intended to serve as the foundation of our identity or a ladder we climb to earn God's approval. Its purpose was always to reveal our deep need—to show us that we cannot save ourselves and to lead us to the one who can.

Jesus met the law's demands head on. Every "you shall," every "you must," every "you better not"—he carried them all the way to Golgotha and nailed them to the cross. As Paul writes, "He forgave us all our sins, having canceled the charge of our legal indebtedness. . . . He has taken it away, nailing it to the cross" (Col. 2:13–14). The Mercy King didn't abolish the law. He fulfilled it on our behalf and then opened the door to freedom.

But for the circumcision party, and others shaped by the same mindset, religion remained a chore to manage, a checklist to maintain. They missed the freedom Christ came to give, settling instead for a harrowing system that could never bring rest.

The film *Parenthood* offers a comical yet poignant glimpse of what that burden feels like. In one memorable scene, Steve Martin's character, an overextended father, is asked by his wife, "Do you have to go?" With a tired sigh he replies, "My whole life is 'have to.'"[2] His words capture the fatigue of a life governed by obligation, where the soul grows weary from doing only what is required, never what is desired. This is the kind of demeanor Paul sees in the Galatians. No wonder he asks them, "What has happened to all of your joy?" (Gal. 4:15).

Into that weariness, G. K. Chesterton has this to say: "Let your religion be less of a theory and more of a love affair."[3]

That is exactly Paul's vision. When faith becomes a response to love rather than a system of pressure, the heart is awakened. Duty gives way to delight. Fear is replaced by joy. Instead of asking, "What must I do to be accepted?" we may even begin asking, "What do I get to do for the one who moved heaven and earth to make me his?"

This isn't a new idea, it's the very heart of the New Covenant. Through the prophet Jeremiah, God promised a day when his law would be written not on stone tablets but on human hearts. "I will put my law in their minds and write it on their hearts. I will be their God, and they will be my people" (Jer. 31:33). This is a secure relationship, a bond sealed not by fear of punishment but by the assurance of belonging.

It's the kind of bond that allows us to say with confidence, "I am my beloved's and my beloved is mine" (Song 6:3). In that relationship, obedience flows not from compulsion but from love. God's wants become our wants. His will becomes our joy. As the weight of shame is lifted, obligation transforms into privilege, and the commands of God begin to feel like invitations rather than chores. This is how we know we're being set free from spiritual Stockholm syndrome. When faith begins to feel like nourishment instead of pressure, when it renews us instead of draining us, we're experiencing what Paul urged the Galatians to rediscover for themselves: freedom rooted in grace.

And yet a gentle warning: The law-bound spirit has a way of lying dormant in us. Like the chickenpox virus, which can resurface years later as shingles, legalism can linger under the surface, waiting for a moment of stress or weakness to flare back up. Its symptoms are familiar: worry, guilt, the deafening whisper of "not enough." For the Galatians these old patterns had reemerged. Paul's mission was to help them put legalism into remission—for good—until the day our risen Mercy King returns and puts it to death once and for all. He wants to do the same for us also.

When we stay tethered to legalism, we inevitably fail to thrive. Faith becomes heartless performance, and joy evaporates. If the voice of "have to" is louder than the invitation of "get to," our hearts grow tired, and we wither and fall from the vine that gives life.

Failure to Thrive: Inferiority and Superiority

Stockholm syndrome of the soul shows up in ways that are as pervasive as they are debilitating. Living under a "have to" burden creates an ongoing inner conflict—swinging between feelings of inferiority and the need to prove superiority. Though these struggles seem opposite, they stem from the same root: a vague, unsettled sense that we don't quite belong, also known as impostor syndrome, and a relentless striving to earn the validation we crave.

Dismantling Inferiority

Most of us know the ache of feeling inferior, like we're on the outside looking in. That quiet whisper, "You don't belong here," can surface in just about any moment.

I remember feeling it acutely at the Country Music Awards, standing in the pit among industry elites and living legends. Patti and I were there thanks to a friend's kindness and a pair of unused A-list tickets. Everyone around us was welcoming, even kind. The woman who won Song of the Year was seated directly in front of us (!). And still I couldn't fully enjoy the moment because I was unable to silence the internal voice reminding me, "You're just here on someone else's pass. Just keep your head down—and don't speak to anyone."

During the event, I shared those feelings with my friend. He smiled and said, "What do you mean you don't belong? You're my friend, my pastor, and you matter to me. I worked hard to get here, and that means I can invite anyone I want. Tonight you and Patti are my guests, and because you're with me, everyone here is glad you're here."

In that moment something inside me let go. I wasn't just included. I was wanted.

That's how grace works. The invitation is always personal, always undeserved, and always tied to someone else's good name. And in the gospel that name is Jesus, the Mercy King. When God looks at us, he doesn't see our résumés or our inadequacies. He sees Christ. We belong because we're with him. Nothing more is needed.

The Galatians had fallen into the same trap of self-doubt and outsider status. Under pressure from misguided gatekeepers, they believed they had to earn their way in, to prove themselves righteous enough to be included in God's family. Without realizing it they had bought a toxic narrative: that they needed their own A-list credentials to belong at the table.

Then the gospel arrived. And changed everything.

Paul's declaration in Galatians 3:28 is revolutionary: "There is neither Jew nor Gentile. . . . You are all one in Christ Jesus." The walls of separation were torn down. Outer court exclusion was dismantled. In Christ every humble, empty-handed soul finds full reception in the courts of the King.

As we've already discovered, this truth spoke powerfully to women in particular—long treated as second-class citizens in society and especially in religious circles. Jesus dignified and lifted them not just through words but through actions. In John 8 the woman caught in adultery is dragged forward for judgment, while her male counterpart is conveniently kept hidden. Jesus steps into that double standard and says to the woman, "I do not condemn you" (John 8:1–11). Paul echoes Jesus' gender-inclusive spirit in a different but no less meaningful way when he writes to the Galatians, "There is neither male nor female"—not just inclusion but co-heirship, full equality, and eternal value.

Paul's words also reached those considered lowest in society's hierarchy: slaves, whose worth had been reduced to property. "There is neither slave nor free." The first conversions to faith in Acts—a woman, a slave girl, and a gentile jailer—further prove that the gospel levels every playing field and obliterates every pecking order.

When Paul writes, "You have put on Christ," he's describing something more than a spiritual upgrade. He's describing a complete reclothing of the soul. With a garment of worth. An identity based no longer on race, class, or gender but on Jesus' mercy. In him everyone belongs and everyone matters.

Dismantling Superiority

If we aren't burdened by inferiority, we may find ourselves striving for superiority. The desire to feel significant is rooted in something good: our image-bearing design. We were created with glory and honor, meant to reflect the greatness of the God who made us (Ps. 8:5). But like so many good things, this longing can be twisted.

The NPR podcast *Hidden Brain* explores this tension in an episode titled "We're All Going to Die." A guest describes how fear of mortality drives many people to seek security through self-importance, a phenomenon he calls "self-esteem striving." We cope with vulnerability by boosting our self-image: "My culture is superior. My nation is best. My religion is the most profound. I am better, smarter, richer."[4]

This bravado is a defense mechanism, a way of shouting over the fear that we don't matter. But it doesn't work. Like the spirit of inferiority, it leaves us hollow.

History gives us countless cautionary tales, and Napoleon Bonaparte is one of them. Rising from obscurity, he built a global empire through intellect and ambition. Yet his confidence masked deep insecurity. He crowned himself emperor, as if to declare that no one stood above him. But his drive to secure personal glory ultimately led to his downfall. The disastrous invasion of Russia, launched in part to protect his legacy, brought immense suffering and ended with Napoleon exiled in disgrace.

Stories like these remind us that when our identity is built on proving we matter, we are never going to find peace. There will always be someone else to beat, another ladder to climb, another title to win. And still the soul remains restless.

The gospel offers better. It frees us from both the fear of not being enough and the exhausting lust to be more. In Christ we no longer strive to earn our place or prove our worth. We've been clothed in his. As Paul writes, "There is neither Jew nor Greek, slave nor free, male nor female." The Mercy King doesn't ask us to qualify for his love. He simply says, "I have called you by name, you are mine" (Isa. 43:1 ESV).

This is the antidote to our failure to thrive. Belonging in Jesus is not contingent on status, strength, or spiritual résumé. It is secured by the one who bore our shame, broke our chains, and calls us his. He isn't just the one who makes space for us, he *is* the space. In Jesus we are home.

Our Way out of Stockholm

Our way out of the captivity of fear, control, and division lies in embracing that the Mercy King has made us his own. His mercy defines the culture of a new kingdom, where belonging is a gift, not a reward. In Christ we belong to God and, through him, to one another. This shared identity reshapes how we see ourselves and how we live in community. It frees us from the chains that once bound us.

The beauty of the church is that it's not a curated group of likeminded individuals. We may choose a church based on familiarity or preference, but once inside, we don't choose who else joins. As relationships deepen and personalities emerge, we sometimes discover that others irritate us—or that we might be the ones who irritate them. People leave. New people arrive. With them come fresh perspectives, different stories, unfamiliar customs. And like the Galatians, we may feel the pull to impose expectations that keep the community feeling more manageable. More like *us*.

But that's not a community. That's a club.

This demand for sameness was at the heart of the Galatian crisis. The ones who were there first—we might call them the founding members—felt threatened and irritated by newcomers who didn't look, act, or worship the way they did. Their solution? Double down. They demanded conformity as the price of admission. Their message was clear: "Follow our rules and customs and we might let you in. But only so far."

Ironically, Paul had once embraced that same mindset. A devout follower of "founder customs," he had defined belonging by purity, pedigree, and performance. But when the Mercy King drew him in, Paul's entire framework collapsed. The one who had once been "a blasphemer and a persecutor and a violent man" (1 Tim. 1:13) was suddenly and forever welcomed, forgiven, and sent out on a new mission: to carry the gospel to those he once considered outsiders.

From that moment forward, Paul's vision and experience of community changed dramatically. In his letters we find him cozying up with those he once would have kept at arm's length: Timothy, an uncircumcised half gentile; Onesimus, a runaway slave; women like Phoebe, a deacon, and Junia, whom he calls an apostle. Paul doesn't just accept these individuals, he mentors them, honors them, learns from them, and entrusts them with the mantle of leadership. These choices and associations cost him friendships and, ultimately, his life.

True Christian community, Paul shows us, is often unexpected, even disruptive. To the outside world, it doesn't make sense. As theologian D. A. Carson puts it, the church is a "band of natural enemies who love one another for Jesus' sake." It includes governors and death row inmates, suburbanites and urbanites, red and blue voters, the affluent and the struggling, the reverent and the recovering. "Red and yellow, black and white"—all are precious in his sight. In the church, Christ's mercy is the glue that holds together what the world tries painstakingly to keep apart.

Paul's vision in Ephesians amplifies that Jesus didn't just reconcile heaven and earth. He reconciled people to one another. "He himself is our peace, who has made the two groups one and has destroyed the barrier, the dividing wall of hostility" (Eph. 2:14). In his death and resurrection, Jesus didn't just make peace possible, he made it real. The Mercy King is the ultimate depolarizer, forming in us a new kind of people within a divided and hostile world. In a cultural moment when disagreement easily escalates into contempt, the church is meant to shine differently. "A gentle answer turns away wrath" (Prov. 15:1). In Christ gentleness becomes a strength.

Many of us in the West forget that we are part of the "ends of the earth" Jesus referred to in his so-called great commission. We are not the center of the Christian story, we are its recipients. We *are* the outsiders who have been brought in, most of us gentiles who once peered in from the temple's outer courts, now welcomed into the very holy of holies. Our faith is built on bequeathed grace, extended to us across centuries and cultures by the faithful witness of others.

It's worth remembering who this Jesus is, the one to whom we've pledged our allegiance. He was a first-century, Middle Eastern, Jewish man. He was brown skinned, poor, often without a home, and he spoke Aramaic. In his own day he was seen as too conservative by some, too liberal by others. He did not fit into anyone's political box. He was an outsider, and he gravitated toward outsiders. He still does.

He calls us beyond our comfort zones, asking, "Am I truly the Savior you want, or would you prefer a smaller world of sameness, safety, and predictability?"

Our smaller selves may hesitate. We may cling to what's comfortable—people who think, act, and vote like we do. But if we are to follow Jesus into the inner courts, we must follow all the way. Disruptions included. After nearly forty years as a Christian and thirty as a pastor, I can say this with confidence: I have never met anyone who regretted taking the disruptive path of the Mercy King. As he said, "Wide is the gate and broad is the road that leads to destruction, and many enter through it. But small is the gate and narrow the road that leads to life, and only a few find it" (Matt. 7:13–14).

We follow the Mercy King not only because he is true but also because he is good, gentle, and better than any other option.

Jesus is better. Always better.

He has reserved seats for us right up front among the A-listers not because we earned them but because he did. And in him, we too become A-listers—fully, joyfully, and eternally. We are let in, and kept in, on his coattails. And there's more still: An after party awaits, the wedding feast of the Lamb. A robust banquet with flowing wine where every man, woman, and child will finally feel what we've longed for all along: to be at home, aware that we are fully known and fully loved.

But we don't have to wait until then.

We can step into that freedom now. We can trade the checklist for communion, the shame for sonship, the burden for belonging. If you hear the voice of the Mercy King today—calling you out of the "have to" life of duty into the "get to" life of love—don't stay shackled one second longer.

Step out. Come in.

The gate is narrow, but the arms of the King are merciful and wide.

Jesus is the Mercy King, and once you've seen his face, remaining in Stockholm, or any place close to it, will seem ridiculous.

Summary

The Galatians had begun to confuse performance with belonging, clinging to rules and religious credentials in the hope of securing what grace had already offered: their place in the family of God. Like hostages growing attached to their captors, they found comfort in the familiar burden of legalism, even when it drained them of joy. Paul's passionate letter calls them—and us—back to the freedom of Christ. Through vivid metaphors, personal stories, and gospel truth, we are invited to trade a life of obligation for one of joyful surrender. In Christ we are not merely pardoned, we are wanted, welcomed, and clothed with honor. The gate may be narrow, but the arms of the Mercy King are merciful and wide.

Three Questions

1. Where in your life do you still feel like a spiritual outsider, unsure whether you really belong unless you prove yourself?
2. Do you tend to carry the weight of inferiority ("I'm not enough") or superiority ("I must be better")? How might the gospel gently confront that tendency in you?
3. What would it look like this week to shift from "have to" to "get to" in your walk with Jesus, living less for validation and more from the delight of being fully known and loved?

One Action Step

Identify one area where you feel pressure to measure up, whether in your faith, relationships, or work. Each morning this week, speak this truth aloud over that place: "I belong because I'm with Jesus." Pair it with a verse like Galatians 4:7: "You are no longer a slave, but God's child." Let this truth interrupt the script of striving, and begin to rewire your heart toward freedom.

TWELVE

When the Grave Feels Final

The Mercy King Who Makes All Things New

> Resurrection means that the worst thing is never the last thing. What is the kingdom of God? A dream? A wish? No, it is what Christ said, what Christ brought, and what he proved.
>
> —Frederick Buechner, *The Final Beast*

Growing up, I had what many would call the ingredients for happiness.

Our home was financially secure. I never worried about meals, and my family enjoyed the comforts of career success. I did well in school, held my own in sports, and had plenty of friends. Yet beneath the surface, a quiet mistrust stirred—of life, of myself, of people around me, even of God. I couldn't name it then, but I was lacking something sturdy and true enough to carry the weight of my doubts, an anchor for the ache I couldn't quite explain.

Years later an older gentleman invited me into a story—and a savior—that would change my life from that point forward. As we opened the Bible together, and as he patiently walked with me through its pages, I discovered a purpose that filled the emptiness I'd carried up to that point. For a time my newfound faith felt whole and unshakable. But as the years passed, doubts crept in—quietly at first, then with more insistence—unraveling the certainty I once held.

Perhaps the doubts were inevitable. People approach faith in different ways. Some see it as a comforting escape from reality. Karl Marx famously called religion "the opiate of the masses," while Mark Twain quipped that it's "believing what you know ain't true." To be fair, and as I've mentioned in previous parts of this book, Christianity's miraculous claims can seem implausible: a virgin birth, water turned to wine, sight restored to the blind, thousands fed with a handful of loaves and fish.

We don't see miracles—or resurrections—every day.

For others, faith is more aesthetic than evidential, an embrace of beauty found in the life of Christ and the stories, teachings, and poetry of Scripture. It's why so much art, literature, and music draw from biblical themes. Dostoyevsky once confessed, "There's nothing lovelier, deeper, more sympathetic, more rational, more manly, and more perfect than Jesus Christ. If someone proved to me that Christ is outside the truth, I would prefer to remain with Christ."[1] For him, Jesus' compelling character outweighed the need for empirical certainty.

For my faith to endure, I knew it had to be more than emotionally stirring or intellectually satisfying. It had to be rooted in truth. What if there really is a creator, a God whose power not only accounts for the wonder of existence but also makes the miracles of Scripture, including the resurrection of Jesus, entirely plausible?

Though I wrestled with deep doubt, unsure whether my belief in the Mercy King would ultimately prove true, I longed with all my heart for it to be so.

It was this same truth that compelled the apostle Paul. Once a skeptic and a fierce opponent of the early church, Paul was radically altered by an encounter with the risen Christ. From that moment on, his message was clear: If Christ has not been raised, then our faith is futile, a comforting illusion at best. But if he has, it changes absolutely everything.

The question that wouldn't let me go was this: Did the resurrection actually happen?

It became the focal point of all my doubts—not just a theological curiosity but a deeply personal search for something solid, something rooted in real time and real space. I wasn't looking for mere inspiration. I needed to know whether death, shame, and despair had truly been conquered. If the resurrection was real, then the story wasn't over—not for Jesus, not for the ones I love, and not for me. Without it my faith would've been little more than shallow sentiment, a wood-rotted crutch for the mind or heart. So I did what felt both terrifying and necessary: I let go of what I thought I knew, and I followed my doubts wherever they led.

What I found surprised me. In chasing my questions, I discovered not the collapse of faith but a deeper, sturdier conviction in the gospel than I had known before. To this day I believe it still: When you lay all the evidence on the table, it takes more faith not to believe in Jesus' resurrection than to believe it.

And as I kept walking that path, I discovered something else, something deeply comforting: I wasn't the first to ask these questions, and I wasn't alone in them. Others, wiser and much farther along than I, had asked the same things and arrived at the same place: The resurrection is not only credible, it is compelling.

If you're wrestling with doubt, especially about the resurrection, take heart. You're not alone, and there are solid answers.

In this final chapter I want to share some of the truths that met me in my own searching, the truths that convinced me that the Mercy King can be trusted fully and that he's worth giving everything for. These truths spoke to the deepest aches and questions of my heart. My prayer is that they will speak to yours as well. Because if Christ isn't risen from the dead, then every chapter before this one is hot air and not worth your time. But if he is risen, the time you have invested to read to this point has not been wasted.

It's All True

The Christian faith makes a bold and extraordinary claim: that Jesus Christ rose bodily from the dead, never to die again, and that this same promise of resurrection awaits all who believe in him. At first glance this seems implausible at best. But a careful, open-minded look at the historical context and eyewitness accounts surrounding that first Easter invites us to consider that faith in the resurrection may not be as farfetched as it sounds.

According to the gospel narratives, several women came to anoint Jesus' body early that Sunday morning, expecting to find his lifeless form sealed in the tomb. Instead they found the stone rolled away, the tomb empty, and a man in white who said, "You seek Jesus of Nazareth, who was crucified. He has risen; he is not here" (Mark 16:6 ESV). They saw it with their own eyes, an absence that became a proclamation. Then they were told to inform Peter and the disciples that they would see Jesus again in Galilee. And they did.

Skeptics might rightly point out that citing the Bible to validate the Bible can feel like circular reasoning. That's a fair concern. But what we have in the resurrection accounts is not just belief, it's testimony. And in any honest evaluation, credible testimony depends not only on what is said but on the reliability and costliness of the witnesses.

Take Peter, for instance. Once full of bravado, then crushed by failure, he later wrote, "We did not follow cleverly devised stories . . . but we were eyewitnesses of his majesty" (2 Peter 1:16). His words come not from someone persuaded by rumor but from one who knew Jesus personally—before and after the resurrection.

Still the modern mind may wonder, "What if these disciples were hallucinating? Grief stricken? Deluded by hope?" That's a valid question too. But history gives us more to consider.

Intelligent Skeptics Who Became Convinced

Over the years, several skeptical intellectuals who set out to disprove the resurrection ended up changing their minds because of where the evidence led.

Frank Morison, a British journalist, began his investigation determined to dismantle the resurrection narrative as legend. But as he dug deeper, the facts refused to cooperate with his assumptions. The more he examined, the more compelled he became by the integrity of the witnesses and the improbability of alternative explanations. What began as a refutation became *Who Moved the Stone?*—a careful defense of the resurrection of Jesus, anchored in historical evidence and eyewitness accounts.[2]

Morison's resistance, like that of many, was not purely intellectual. It was also personal. Doubt often serves as a shield against disappointment. But in seeking truth, he found not cold conclusions but a warm invitation to trust.

C. S. Lewis took a similar path. A brilliant Oxford scholar and once self-described reluctant convert, Lewis wrestled with the intellectual tensions of faith for years. Influenced by Christian thinkers like G. K. Chesterton and George MacDonald and challenged by conversations with Christian friends like J. R. R. Tolkien, Lewis eventually acknowledged that Christianity made sense not only emotionally but logically. "A young man who wishes to remain a sound atheist cannot be too careful of his reading," he famously wrote.[3] In the end, like Morison, Lewis concluded that it requires more faith to reject the resurrection than to embrace it.

In some circles Christian faith is dismissed as naïve or anti-intellectual. But stories like these suggest otherwise. Many thoughtful people—past and present—have come to faith not by abandoning reason but by following it. Real faith doesn't ignore or suppress the intellect. It engages and uses it. It asks hard questions, weighs evidence, and, like Thomas, sometimes comes to belief through the avenue of expressing honest doubt and asking the Mercy King for more.

Jesus' response to Thomas is worth noticing. He doesn't shame or belittle him for needing more. Instead he meets him with patience and offers exactly what Thomas asks for. That moment wasn't just for Thomas. It's a picture of how Jesus meets all of us in our questions. And his words still speak today: "Because you have seen me, you have believed; blessed are those who have not seen and yet have believed" (John 20:24–29).

If you find yourself in a funk, calling everything into question, you're not out of place. The invitation still stands: Bring your doubts, follow them honestly, and see where they lead. You're not asked to silence your thinking, only to be open to where it might take you.

It's All Beautiful

For many who affirm Christianity on intellectual grounds, another hurdle often remains: an aesthetic one. They are drawn to the beauty of Christ—his love, his mercy, his wisdom—yet disheartened when that same beauty seems absent in the lives of those who claim to follow him. This gap between the teachings of Jesus and the conduct of his people—what some call hypocrisy—can be one of the most painful barriers to belief.

Frederick Douglass knew this tension well. Born into slavery, Douglass found deep inspiration in the gospel's message of justice and liberation. At the same time, he bore witness to the stark contrast between the way of Jesus and the distorted Christianity practiced by many in his day. In his autobiography, *Narrative of the Life of Frederick Douglass*, he writes, "Between the Christianity of this land and the Christianity of Christ, I recognize the widest possible difference."[4]

Douglass saw men who professed faith while defending oppression, pastors who preached grace but turned a blind eye to cruelty. Though he never rejected Christ, he wrestled deeply with the ways that Christian faith had been misrepresented by those who held power. His experience echoes a struggle many still face today: how to hold on to the beauty of Jesus while wrestling with the painful inconsistency of his followers.

Francis Schaeffer, a pastor and philosopher who founded the L'Abri Fellowship, faced a similar crisis of disillusionment. During his early years in ministry, he noticed a disturbing pattern: Many of his fellow Presbyterian pastors, though doctrinally sound and theologically sharp, were notably competitive with and harsh in spirit toward one another. Instead of exhibiting the gentleness and humility of Christ, they often engaged in slander, gossip, turf wars, and bitter rivalry. They were, in Schaeffer's own words, "mean as snakes."

This disconnection between orthodoxy and love broke his heart. If, Schaeffer wondered, the truth of Christianity doesn't produce beauty in its adherents, is it really true at all? The dissonance cut deeply enough that he stepped away from ministry for a time and, in his own words, "started at the beginning." He reexamined the claims of Christianity, tested other worldviews, and searched the Scriptures not as a teacher but as a seeker and skeptic. It was a season of quiet wrestling laced with doubt and prayer, solitude and tears.

After weeks of this soul-searching, he came to a quiet but firm realization. Turning to his wife, Edith, he said simply and sincerely, "There's one reason and only one reason to be a Christian: because it's all true."[5]

His renewed conviction wasn't rooted in the perfect behavior of Christians; it was rooted in the perfect beauty of Jesus, the Mercy King. And from that place, Schaeffer would go on to shape generations of doubters, skeptics, and believers with a deep, unmistakable love that bore witness to the grace of the one he came once again to trust and follow.

If you've struggled to engage Christianity because of the hypocrisy you've seen in Christians, you're not alone. But let me gently suggest this: Is it fair—or intellectually honest—to dismiss Jesus Christ because some who claim him as Lord and Savior fall short? This doesn't excuse sins like the ones Schaeffer encountered in his fellow pastors, nor does it diminish the damage done by those egregious failures. But it does remind us that the best way to evaluate Christ is not by the worst examples of his followers but by his own life, his own claims, and his own unmatched track record of perfect truth, beauty, goodness, and love.

The appeal of Christianity can sometimes feel elusive, especially when set against the backdrop of its darkest chapters or the personal failings of those who bear its name. One might understandably ask, "How can a faith be good when so much harm has been done in its name?" From the violence of the Crusades to the misuse of Scripture to justify slavery, from church-sanctioned oppression to scandals involving leaders who fall without repentance—these wounds are real, and they matter.

Such questions deserve more than quick answers; they call for honest reckoning. They also place a clear responsibility on those who follow Jesus: to live with integrity, humility, and love, embodying the likeness of the one we profess to know, love, and follow.

This begins with distinguishing true Christianity from its counterfeits. Anything abusive, manipulative, or mean spirited may claim Christ's name, but it does not reflect his heart. As Peter exhorts, "Live such good lives among the pagans that . . . they may see your good deeds and glorify God" (1 Peter 2:12). Jesus envisioned his people as light—visible not through self-righteousness or loud proclamations but through a quiet goodness that refreshes the world.

When Christians fail to add beauty, kindness, and hope to their surroundings, something essential is missing. Our presence should be a blessing, even to those who disagree with us. Madeleine L'Engle captured this vision well when she described the Christian witness as "a light that is so lovely that [people] cannot help but ask the source of that light."[6] Rather than finger-pointing or fearmongering, authentic faith in the Mercy King draws others in by the loveliness of its—and his—fruit.

There are countless examples of this—far too many to name. While not everything good in the world comes from Christians, followers of Jesus have often been at the forefront of healing and renewal: building orphanages, abolishing slavery, advancing civil rights, caring for the poor, and giving generously—and sacrificially—for the common good.

If Jesus were to walk through my city of Nashville—a hub for health care—I imagine he might smile at the legacy of hospitals and health systems started by people who saw physical, emotional, and psychological healing as part of the Mercy King's calling on their lives. The same could be said of many schools, nonprofits, works of art, efforts in government, and everyday acts of quiet neighbor love that go unseen in this wonderful city of ours. They may not make headlines, but they reflect the heart of the Mercy King all the same.

Yet sometimes they do make headlines. Nicholas Kristof, an agnostic journalist and humanitarian, once wrote in *The New York Times*, "In certain circles, Christians constitute one of the few groups that it's safe to mock openly. Yet the negative caricature is incomplete and unfair. I have little in common politically or theologically with Christians, but I've been truly awed by those I've seen in so many remote places, combating illiteracy and warlords, famine and disease, humbly struggling to do the Lord's work as they see it."[7]

Kristof's words echo what many have seen with their own eyes: In the most forgotten corners of the world, it is often Christians who stay after others have gone—serving, healing, feeding, and holding space for hope. They become the Mercy King's ambassadors in places where mercy is needed most.

For every public Christian failure we rightly grieve, there are, in every generation, hundreds of thousands of untold stories, quiet lives shaped by faithfulness, humility, and love. One of Christianity's most beautiful virtues is just that: humility. And perhaps that's why these stories are so often overlooked and go unseen. But maybe they shouldn't be.

Jesus said "let your light shine before others" not so we might be seen but so his character and goodness shining through us might be. Every day, Christians across the world step into a life of love—serving quietly, advocating for justice, lifting burdens from weary shoulders. Perhaps our greatest shortcoming isn't that we do too little but that too little is said about the good that love in Christ's name is quietly bringing to life all around us.

It's All Going to Be Okay

The gospel has always resonated most deeply with those who are painfully aware of their limitations, weaknesses, and wounds—not the powerful or the polished but the ones who know their need for the King's mercy. As we reflect on the resurrection, we find that it brings hope and healing in some of the most unexpected places—especially to the discarded, the damaged, the defeated, and even the dead.

Discarded People Are Made Prominent

As we have covered at length in this book—but it bears repeating—in Jesus' time, society often overlooked the voices of women, the poor, the sick, the disabled, and outsiders. In a deeply patriarchal culture, Jesus chose women as the first witnesses of his resurrection. The angel at the empty tomb didn't just comfort them, he sent them: "Go and tell the disciples that he is risen." They weren't only invited to see, they were given authority from on high to speak and preach in his name.

This moment turns social hierarchies on their heads. And it wasn't just women. Throughout his ministry, Jesus elevated those the culture ignored. He touched lepers, dined with the poor, welcomed gentiles, forgave and elevated scandalous sinners, and gave voice to the marginalized. As a friend of mine once said, "The stone was rolled away not to let Jesus out but to let every type of person in." From the very start, the resurrection signaled a radically inclusive kingdom. In God's family no one is discardable, only deeply known, deeply loved, and elevated with dignity. This is one way the Mercy King wields power: by lifting up those the world pushes down.

Damaged People Are Made Fruitful

Mary Magdalene—one of the women at the tomb—had once been tormented by seven demons. In the eyes of her community, she likely was viewed as unstable or dangerous. A person to avoid. But Jesus saw through the stigma and into her story. He healed her, and then entrusted her with one of the greatest honors in all of history: to be the first among the women to proclaim his resurrection.

Before that morning, Mary was known only for her afflictions. After that morning, she became known for hope. Her story is a reminder that Jesus doesn't merely heal what is broken, he gives it purpose. Her life testifies to what many of us ache to believe: that the damaged parts of us do not disqualify us from being loved and used by God. That they may be the very places he chooses to work through most.

I think of a small group I once formed with my friend Chris, who makes his living as a painter and musician. We called ourselves "the Knuckleheads"—a space to be honest about our flaws and open about our need for grace. One night Chris, who lives with a persistent sense of restlessness, said something that has stayed with me: "If you gave me the option to lose my restlessness, I'd say no. My best creativity depends on it." His words echo Mary's story: that God doesn't work around our weaknesses, he works through them.

Defeated People Are Restored

The resurrection also speaks powerfully to those who feel defined by failure. Peter, who had once vowed unwavering loyalty to Jesus, denied him three times during his darkest hour. The shame of his betrayal must have been crushing—a single moment of cowardice seeming to erase years of connection and commitment. And yet when the angel at the tomb delivered the message of the resurrection, it came with a personal addendum: "Go, tell his disciples and Peter" (Mark 16:7). That small phrase—"and Peter"—is a glimpse into Jesus' tender heart. Peter wasn't sidelined or shamed. He was sought out.

The resurrection doesn't cancel us for our worst moments. It restores us. Peter, the cowardly denier, would become a leader in the early church known especially for his courage. The Mercy King does not erase our past. Instead he redeems it and reassigns us.

Dead People Are Given a Future

Finally, the resurrection speaks to the deepest fear we carry: of death itself. Outside of Christ, life can feel like a slow march toward a closing door. But Jesus broke that door off its hinges. He didn't just conquer death for himself; he extended the promise of new, eternal life to all who trust in him. His resurrection from the grave is, as Scripture assures us, "the firstfruits of those who have fallen asleep. . . . For as in Adam all die, so in Christ all will be made alive" (1 Cor. 15:20–26).

Our friend Joni Eareckson Tada, who has lived for decades with paralysis, embodies this hope with bold and defiant optimism. She often says that when she gets to heaven, she plans to stand up, walk to Jesus, and thank him. And then, with joy, she'll place her wheelchair in a corner of heaven and say, "Lord, for decades, I was pushed around in that chair—but thank you for using it to draw me close to you. It was a gift that helped me rely on you." For Joni the chair will be retired, but not forgotten. It will stand as a symbol of God's mercy in suffering, a reminder of how the Mercy King pursues and meets us not in spite of our pain but right in the middle of it.[8]

The End Becomes the Beginning of Life

The hope of the resurrection reaches far beyond our present trials. It stretches not only to the end of time but into eternity itself. Jesus' resurrection was never meant to be a fleeting triumph or a miraculous footnote; it was the unveiling of a promise, the turning point of history, and the doorway to personal access. A creator-redeemer declaring that all things broken, including you and me, will one day be made whole. In rising from the dead, Jesus did more than conquer the grave; he established himself as the true and eternal King, initiating the great restoration of all things under his reign of mercy.

The resurrection is the exclamation point of divine mercy, proof that the Mercy King not only overcomes death but delights to spread his mercy far and wide, reaching into the lives of the discarded, the damaged, the defeated, and even the dead.

As Matthew's gospel tenderly reminds us, Jesus rose "just as he said," a tender yet powerful assurance that every word he has spoken, every promise he has made, has come to pass and will continue to do so. In John's gospel Jesus declares, "I am the resurrection and the life. Whoever believes in me, though he die, yet shall he live" (John 11:25 ESV). This is our assurance: When Christ returns, all who have died in him will also rise to a world without death, mourning, crying, or pain (Rev. 21:1–8), a world where we will be like him, for we will see him as he truly is (1 John 3:2).

Dietrich Bonhoeffer held tightly to this promise in his final days. Imprisoned by the Nazis for his role in resisting Hitler, he spent his remaining time encouraging fellow prisoners, pointing them again and again to the hope of resurrection. On the morning of April 9, 1945, as he was led to the gallows, he turned to a fellow inmate and said, "This is the end—for me, the beginning of life."[9] The pastor and martyr's confidence in Christ's victory over death never wavered. What's more, it was emboldened as it became more costly.

Bonhoeffer had long understood that faith in Christ meant surrendering everything—even his life—into God's hands. In *Letters and Papers from Prison*, he writes, "Death is the supreme festival on the road to freedom. . . . God lets us know that we must not think of death as the end, but rather as the path to perfect liberation, to the redemption of our whole being. It is grace to know this, and to be able to die knowing it."[10]

One of the guards who witnessed his execution later remarked on the peace and assurance Bonhoeffer displayed, even in his final moments. He walked to his death with calm resolve, as though he were merely stepping into a greater reality.[11]

Dietrich Bonhoeffer was only thirty-nine years old when he died, yet his execution, intended as a final defeat, stands as a testament to an ironic victory for poetic justice: a life cut short that paradoxically guaranteed the enduring power of his faith and message.

Bonhoeffer's story reminds us that resurrection hope is not just a comfort in life but a firm foundation in the face of death. As Paul writes, "Neither death nor life . . . nor anything else in all creation, will be able to separate us from the love of God that is in Christ Jesus our Lord" (Rom. 8:38–39). Bonhoeffer lived and died as if that promise were already true—and it was.

If you, like Bonhoeffer, have placed your trust in the risen Christ, then you already carry a hope stronger than death and more enduring than any sorrow. And if you're still wrestling—still unsure, still aching for something solid—if the quiet cry of your heart is, "God, have mercy on me," then take heart: Jesus has a soft spot for those who struggle. He gently moves toward you, mercifully reassures you, and seeks to embolden you with reminders that the tomb is empty and it awaits you as a witness.

So lean in. Ask your questions. Bring all that you have and are to his merciful feet, at the foot of his merciful throne. Draw near to God and he will draw near to you (James 4:8).

It will be the bravest—as well as the smartest—move you'll ever make.

Summary

Jesus' resurrection is not just the hinge of history, it is the heartbeat of hope for every discarded, damaged, defeated, and dying soul. Historically credible, emotionally healing, and theologically rich, the empty tomb declares that the Mercy King has conquered death with love, and he continues to spread that mercy far and wide. For all who feel unqualified, unsure, or undone, the risen Christ extends a deeply personal invitation: Come as you are. Nothing is wasted, no one is too far gone, and in him, everything—one day—will be made new.

Three Questions

1. Where do you most feel your need for mercy right now, and how does the resurrection speak specifically to that ache?
2. Which story from this chapter—Mary Magdalene's transformation, Peter's restoration, Bonhoeffer's confidence, or your own life—most mirrors where you are with faith today?
3. What would it look like to live as if resurrection hope were already true in your ordinary, everyday relationships?

One Action Step

Identify one place in your life that feels like a tomb—an unresolved regret, a quiet shame, a lingering doubt—and write it down. Then in prayer invite the Mercy King to meet you there, not with polished words but with honest surrender. This week take one small step to embody resurrection hope in someone else's life: Offer a word of grace, a listening ear, or an unexpected act of kindness. Let the mercy that found you ripple outward.

Conclusion

He's Still Running Toward You

This is not the end of something but only the beginning.

Jesus' mercy isn't meant to stay on the page. It's meant to reach into your real, everyday life—to shape how you think, how you relate, how you persevere, and how you hope. Mercy is not abstract. It's real. It's active. And it moves toward you with strength and compassion.

Throughout this book, we've looked at the longings we carry, the wounds we bear, and the hope that holds us together. These aren't just spiritual themes, they're the fabric of life. Jesus doesn't offer a detour around our struggles, he offers himself in the middle of them. The places where you still feel weak, weary, or unfinished are not obstacles to his mercy. They are the places where his mercy meets you most personally.

Jesus is not waiting for you to become someone else. He's not holding back affection until you demonstrate progress and show that you get it. He is already with you. He is already for you. His love has never been reluctant.

This is who he is. Jesus, the Mercy King, is the shepherd who leaves the ninety-nine to go after the one. The friend of sinners. The savior who draws near to the broken and carries the weary. His power doesn't crush, it restores. There is no part of your story he cannot reach. Not the shame you carry. Not the questions you haven't found answers for. Not the seasons that still feel like failure. His mercy is wide enough and deep enough for it all.

To live tethered to Jesus means living honestly—with God, with others, and with yourself. You don't have to pretend or hide. The safest place for your weakness and the worst true things about you is in the hands of the one who already bore it all at the cross. It also means letting grace, not pressure, shape your understanding of who God is. When you fall short, you don't start over. You return. Grace isn't earned, and it isn't lost. His invitation remains: "Come to me."

As mercy becomes more real to you, it will also change how you see and treat others. You'll stop measuring people by performance and status. You'll start seeing them as fellow image-bearers just as in need of grace as you are.

You no longer have to prove your worth. You are not on trial. You are not defined by your performance or reputation. You are defined by the one who calls you his beloved. The world will keep pushing for more—more effort, more achievement, more strength. But Jesus speaks a better word: "My grace is sufficient for you. My power is made perfect in weakness."

So as we finish our time together here, I pray you will stay close to him. Let his mercy ground you. Let his voice shape your soul. Let his presence anchor you through each day and season. And when you forget—because you will—come back. He's not keeping score. He awaits your return, even as he runs toward you.

Because running to redeem, restore, and receive his beloved is what the Mercy King does.

And he's not finished with you yet.

More from Scott

To inquire about scheduling Scott for any of the following, please visit *scottsauls.com*:

- Speaking inquiries for events, churches, orgs, and teams
- Leader cohorts and mentoring
- Team enrichment

To receive Scott's weekly essay in your inbox, subscribe at *scottsauls.substack.com*.

To receive Scott's twice-weekly teaching, subscribe to *That's a Great Question* on *YouTube.com/scottsauls* or on Apple or Spotify Podcasts.

Notes

Chapter 1: When You Feel Too Broken to Belong

1. G. K. Chesterton, *Orthodoxy* (John Lane Company, 1908), 47.
2. Charles Haddon Spurgeon, "God's Mercy to the Chief of Sinners," sermon no. 91, preached June 22, 1856, at New Park Street Chapel, Southwark. In *The New Park Street Pulpit*, vol. 2 (Passmore and Alabaster, 1856).
3. D. T. Niles, *That They May Have Life* (Abingdon, 1951), 96.
4. Mahatma Gandhi, *An Autobiography: The Story of My Experiments with Truth*, trans. Mahadev Desai (Dover, 1983), 234.
5. John Bunyan, *Grace Abounding to the Chief of Sinners* (Banner of Truth, 2016), 35–37.
6. C. S. Lewis, *Mere Christianity* (HarperCollins, 2001), 137.
7. Lewis, *Mere Christianity*, 136.
8. Alistair Begg, "The Man on the Middle Cross Said I Could Come," sermon preached at Parkside Church, Bainbridge, OH. Truth for Life, November 20, 2019. Available at Truth for Life and on YouTube.
9. Martin Luther, *The Freedom of a Christian* (Fortress, 2008), 50.

Chapter 2: When Power Fails You

1. Algernon Charles Swinburne, "Hymn of Man," in *Songs Before Sunrise* (Chatto and Windus, 1871), 45.
2. C. S. Lewis, *The Great Divorce* (HarperCollins, 1946), 98–101.

3. Henri J. M. Nouwen, *The Road to Daybreak: A Spiritual Journey* (Doubleday, 1988), 143–45.
4. Francis A. Schaeffer, *No Little People* (Crossway, 2003), 13.
5. Tim Rice and Andrew Lloyd Webber, "Pilate's Dream," *Jesus Christ Superstar* (MCA Records, 1970).
6. Paul David Tripp, *New Morning Mercies: A Daily Gospel Devotional* (Crossway, 2014), November 2.

Chapter 3: When Your Heart Has Been Hijacked

1. John Calvin, *Institutes of the Christian Religion*, trans. Henry Beveridge (Calvin Translation Society, 1845), book 1, chapter 6, section 8.
2. Augustine, *Confessions*, trans. Henry Chadwick (Oxford University Press, 1991), 3.
3. C. S. Lewis, *Mere Christianity* (HarperCollins, 2001), 50.
4. Origen, *Homilies on Exodus, Leviticus, Numbers*, trans. Ronald E. Heine (Catholic University of America Press, 1982), 74.
5. David F. Wells, *Losing Our Virtue: Why the Church Must Recover Its Moral Vision* (Eerdmans, 1998), 4.
6. Fred Hoyle, *The Intelligent Universe: A New View of Creation and Evolution* (Holt, Rinehart, and Winston, 1983), 19.
7. David Foster Wallace, "This Is Water," commencement address, Kenyon College, Gambier, OH, May 21, 2005.
8. Brené Brown, *The Gifts of Imperfection: Let Go of Who You Think You're Supposed to Be and Embrace Who You Are* (Hazelden, 2010), 25.

Chapter 4: When Comparison Steals Your Joy

1. Ethan Kross et al., "Facebook Use Predicts Declines in Subjective Well-Being in Young Adults," *PLoS ONE* 8, no. 8 (2013): e69841, https://doi.org/10.1371/journal.pone.0069841.
2. Jean M. Twenge et al., "Increases in Depressive Symptoms, Suicide-Related Outcomes, and Suicide Rates Among U.S. Adolescents After 2010 and Links to Increased New Media Screen Time," *Clinical Psychological Science* 6, no. 1 (2017): 3–17, https://doi.org/10.1177/2167702617723376.

3. Zig Ziglar, *Over the Top: Moving from Survival to Stability, from Stability to Success, from Success to Significance* (Thomas Nelson, 1997), n.p.
4. James Robert Boyd, *Elements of Moral Philosophy, for the Use of Schools* (Clark and Hesser, 1875), 226.
5. Paul David Tripp, *Instruments in the Redeemer's Hands: People in Need of Change Helping People in Need of Change* (P & R Publishing, 2002), 52.
6. John F. Helliwell et al., eds., *World Happiness Report 2025* (Wellbeing Research Centre, University of Oxford, 2025), www.worldhappiness.report/ed/2025.
7. C. S. Lewis, *Mere Christianity* (HarperCollins, 2001), 122.
8. Jonathan Edwards, *The "Miscellanies," 501–832*, ed. Ava Chamberlain, vol. 18 of *The Works of Jonathan Edwards*, ed. Harry S. Stout (Yale University Press, 2000), 83.
9. *Demi Lovato: Simply Complicated*, documentary, directed by Jeff Bierman et al. (SB Projects, 2017).
10. Joseph Epstein, *Envy: The Seven Deadly Sins* (Oxford University Press, 2003), 3.
11. Arthur C. Brooks, "Love People, Not Pleasure," *The New York Times*, July 18, 2014, www.nytimes.com/2014/07/20/opinion/sunday/arthur-c-brooks-love-people-not-pleasure.html.
12. Horatio G. Spafford, "It Is Well with My Soul" (1873), in *The United Methodist Hymnal* (United Methodist Publishing House, 1989), no. 377.
13. C. S. Lewis, *The Weight of Glory* (HarperOne, 2001), 45.
14. Dietrich Bonhoeffer, *God Is in the Manger: Reflections on Advent and Christmas*, trans. O. C. Dean Jr. (Westminster John Knox, 2010), 85.

Chapter 5: When Suffering Shakes Your Faith

1. J. R. R. Tolkien, *The Return of the King* (Houghton Mifflin Harcourt, 2005), 135.
2. C. S. Lewis, *The Weight of Glory and Other Addresses* (HarperOne, 2001), 26.

3. Tom Petty, "The Waiting," *Hard Promises* (Backstreet Records, 1981).
4. *1883*, created by Taylor Sheridan, performances by Tim McGraw and Faith Hill, season 1, episode 1, (Paramount+, 2021).
5. Timothy Keller, *Walking with God Through Pain and Suffering* (Riverhead, 2013), 185.
6. Tolkien, *Return of the King*, 246.

Chapter 6: When You Can't Forgive Yourself

1. Jennie Jerome, quoted in "The Great Rivalry, as Told by Punch," *Gladstone's Library*, October 24, 2017, www.gladstoneslibrary.org.
2. Leo Tolstoy, *A Confession*, trans. Aylmer Maude (Dover, 2006), 80.
3. *World's Greatest Dad*, directed by Bobcat Goldthwait (Magnolia Pictures, 2009), spoken by Robin Williams' character, Lance Clayton.
4. Brené Brown, *The Gifts of Imperfection: Let Go of Who You Think You're Supposed to Be and Embrace Who You Are* (Hazelden, 2010), 26.
5. Dr. Seuss, *How the Grinch Stole Christmas!* (Random House, 1957), n.p.

Chapter 7: When Religion Beats You Down

1. *Chariots of Fire*, directed by Hugh Hudson, performances by Ian Charleson and Ben Cross (Warner Brothers, 1981).
2. William Temple, *Readings in St. John's Gospel* (Macmillan, 1952), 58.
3. Timothy Keller with Kathy Keller, *The Meaning of Marriage: Facing the Complexities of Commitment with the Wisdom of God* (Riverhead, 2011), 226.
4. Walter Brueggemann, *Sabbath as Resistance: Saying No to the Culture of Now* (Westminster John Knox, 2014), 31.
5. Popular saying frequently attributed to Anne Lamott, but without a verifiable primary source.
6. Claire Diaz-Ortiz, *Design Your Day: Be More Productive, Set Better Goals, and Live Life on Purpose* (Moody, 2015), 26.

7. Charles H. Spurgeon, *The Treasury of David* (Marshall, Morgan, and Scott, 1980), 79.
8. John Newton, *Olney Hymns* (1779), hymn 35.

Chapter 8: When Ruthless Trust Is Your Only Option

1. Brennan Manning, *Ruthless Trust: The Ragamuffin's Path to God* (HarperSanFrancisco, 2000).
2. C. S. Lewis, *Mere Christianity* (HarperCollins, 2001), 208.
3. Os Guinness, *God in the Dark: The Assurance of Faith Beyond a Shadow of Doubt* (Crossway, 1996), 52.
4. G. K. Chesterton, *The Autobiography of G. K. Chesterton* (Sheed and Ward, 1936), 212.
5. Francis A. Schaeffer, *He Is There and He Is Not Silent* (Tyndale, 1972), 27.
6. Fleming Rutledge, *The Crucifixion: Understanding the Death of Jesus Christ* (Eerdmans, 2015), 443.

Chapter 9: When You're Tired of Pretending

1. Michael Phelps, interview by David Axelrod, *The Axe Files*, CNN, January 20, 2018.
2. Julie Brown Patton, "Olympian Michael Phelps Divulges 'Purpose Driven Life' Saved Him from Suicide, Revealed God," *Gospel Herald*, August 6, 2016.
3. Martin Luther, "Preface to the Complete Edition of His Latin Works (1545)," in *Luther's Works* (Fortress, 1960), vol. 34, 336–37.
4. "Daily Affirmation with Stuart Smalley," *Saturday Night Live*, season 17, episode 5, aired November 16, 1991, on NBC.
5. Babylonian Talmud, *Menachot* 43b.
6. Victor Hugo, *Les Misérables*, trans. Norman Denny (Penguin Classics, 1982), n.p.
7. Barna Group, "Pastors Share Top Reasons They've Considered Quitting Ministry in the Past Year," *Barna.com*, April 27, 2022, www.barna.com/research/pastors-quitting-ministry.
8. John Lynch, "Oprah Says Every Guest Asks Her the Same

Question After Their Interview—but She Was Still Shocked When Beyoncé Asked It," *Business Insider*, September 25, 2017, www.businessinsider.com/oprah-winfrey-question-every-guests-asks-after-interviews-beyonce-2017-9.

9. Hilary Weaver, "Oprah Winfrey Had Trouble Adjusting to Life After Her Talk Show," *Vanity Fair*, April 13, 2017, www.vanityfair.com/style/2017/04/oprah-winfrey-had-trouble-adjusting-to-life-after-talk-show.
10. I first heard this term used by Tim Keller.
11. Ernest Hemingway, *A Farewell to Arms* (Scribner, 2012), 216.
12. James Montgomery Boice, *Romans: The Reign of Grace* (Baker, 1992), 113.
13. Fleming Rutledge, *The Crucifixion: Understanding the Death of Jesus Christ* (Eerdmans, 2015), 589.

Chapter 10: When You Have Nothing Left to Give

1. *Dumb and Dumber*, directed by Peter Farrelly, performances by Jim Carrey and Jeff Daniels (New Line Cinema, 1994).
2. Dietrich Bonhoeffer, *The Cost of Discipleship* (Macmillan, 1937), 45–49.
3. John Stott, *The Message of Ephesians: God's New Society* (InterVarsity Press, 1979), 72–73.
4. James Montgomery Boice, *Romans: The Reign of Grace* (Baker, 1992), 113.
5. Martin Luther, *Lectures on Romans*, trans. Wilhelm Pauck (Westminster John Knox, 2006), 195.
6. *Wonder*, directed by Stephen Chbosky (Lionsgate, 2017).
7. John Donne, *Holy Sonnets*, sonnet 14, in *John Donne: The Major Works*, ed. John Carey (Oxford University Press, 1990), 285.

Chapter 11: When You're Stuck in Stockholm

1. F. Scott Fitzgerald, *The Great Gatsby* (Scribner, 2004), 90–92.
2. *Parenthood*, directed by Ron Howard, performances by Steve Martin and Mary Steenburgen (Universal Pictures, 1989).

3. G. K. Chesterton, *The Collected Works of G. K. Chesterton* (Ignatius, 1986), 256.
4. Shankar Vedantam et al., "We're All Gonna Die! How Fear of Death Drives Our Behavior," *Hidden Brain*, NPR, September 13, 2019, www.npr.org/2019/09/13/760599683/were-all-gonna-die-how-fear-of-death-drives-our-behavior.

Chapter 12: When the Grave Feels Final

1. Fyodor Dostoyevsky, *The Brothers Karamazov*, trans. Constance Garnett (Lowell Press, 1912), 78.
2. Frank Morison, *Who Moved the Stone?* (Faber and Faber, 1930), 1–3.
3. C. S. Lewis, *Surprised by Joy: The Shape of My Early Life* (Harcourt, Brace, 1955), 237.
4. Frederick Douglass, *Narrative of the Life of Frederick Douglass, an American Slave, Written by Himself* (Anti-Slavery Office, 1845), 95.
5. Francis A. Schaeffer, *The God Who Is There* (InterVarsity Press, 1968), 19.
6. Madeleine L'Engle, *Walking on Water: Reflections on Faith and Art* (Harold Shaw, 1980), 92.
7. Nicholas Kristof, "A Little Respect for Dr. Foster," *The New York Times*, March 28, 2015, www.nytimes.com/2015/03/29/opinion/sunday/nicholas-kristof-a-little-respect-for-dr-foster.html.
8. Joni Eareckson Tada, *Heaven: Your Real Home from a Higher Perspective* (Zondervan, 1995), 5–6.
9. Eric Metaxas, *Bonhoeffer: Pastor, Martyr, Prophet, Spy* (Thomas Nelson, 2010), 527.
10. Dietrich Bonhoeffer, *Letters and Papers from Prison*, trans. Reginald H. Fuller (Macmillan, 1971), 391.
11. Eberhard Bethge, *Dietrich Bonhoeffer: A Biography*, rev. and ed. Victoria J. Barnett (Fortress, 2000), 927.

From the Publisher

GREAT BOOKS

ARE EVEN BETTER WHEN THEY'RE SHARED!

Help other readers find this one

- Post a review at your favorite online bookseller
- Post a picture on a social media account and share why you enjoyed it
- Send a note to a friend who would also love it—or better yet, give them a copy

Thanks for reading!